Praise for *Why Don't You W*

"It's the relationship, stupid! You[r] [   ]
for anything if you fail to under[stand] [   ]
relationship. That's why I highly recommend Rick Maurer's
book. It shows you how to pay attention to your idea and
the other person at the same time."

Jeff Perkins
SVP Human Resources
AOL Europe

"*Why Don't You Want What I Want?* pr[ovides a] [   ]
way to understand and work with resistance to change.
The models and recommended actions are meaningful
to engineers and change leaders alike."

Candice L. Phelan
Director of Learning Services
Lockheed Martin Corporation

"Rick Maurer presents a practical guide for anyone who
wants to build support for new ideas quickly. He reminds
readers that agreements and successful changes start with
solid relationships — essential in conducting business
with integrity. A succinct, useful, and common-sense
approach."

John W. Loose
CEO
Corning Inc.

"Maurer gets it right. One of the best ways to reward and
energize people is to pay attention to their ideas and
concerns. This book shows you how to advance your own
ideas while incorporating the best thinking of others."

Bob Nelson
author, *1001 Ways to Reward Employees* and
Please Don't Just Do What I Tell You, Do What Needs to Be Done

"Rick's book gives leaders great examples, workable tools, and clear explanations of what works and what doesn't work when presenting ideas. It will help you to influence, in a positive way, a diverse group of stakeholders inside and outside your organization."

Jolene Tornabeni
Executive Vice Presdent/COO
Inova Health System

"*Why Don't You Want What I Want?* helps illuminate communication and success. It shows all of us how we can ethically and effectively marshal our social influence for the betterment of our careers, our teams, and our organizations."

Othon Herrera
President & COO
IntelliMark

"Read Rick's book — it's filled with great ideas and techniques to help you get what you want. And you'll laugh and 'aha' along the way too! It offers practical, field-tested advice to help you exceed your expectations."

Mark Victor Hansen
co-author, *Chicken Soup for the Soul* series

"The ideas in this book really work. They have helped our executive team see the complexity of the interactions that were blocking us and become much more effective."

Donald T. Floyd, Jr.
President and CEO
National 4-H Council

Why Don't You Want What I Want?

Also by Rick Maurer

Building Capacity for Change Sourcebook
Tools for Leading Major Changes Effectively

Beyond the Wall of Resistance
*Unconventional Strategies That Build
Support for Change*

Caught in the Middle
*A Leadership Guide for Partnership
in the Workplace*

Feedback Toolkit
*Sixteen Tools for Better Communication
in the Workplace*

Why Don't You Want What I Want?

*How to
Win Support
for Your Ideas
without
Hard Sell,
Manipulation,
or Power Plays*

Rick Maurer

Austin • Atlanta

Why Don't You Want What I Want?

How to Win Support for Your Ideas without
Hard Sell, Manipulation, or Power Plays

Rick Maurer

Bard Press
An imprint of Longstreet Press
2974 Hardman Court
Atlanta, GA 30305
404-254-0110 voice, 404-254-0116 fax
www.bardpress.com

To order the book, contact your local bookstore or call 800-945-3132.

ISBN 1-885167-56-3 paperback

Library of Congress Cataloging-in-Publication Data
Maurer, Rick.
    Why don't you want what I want? : how to win support for
    your ideas without hard sell, manipulation, or power plays /
    Rick Maurer.
        p.   cm.
    Includes index.
    ISBN 1-885167-56-3 (trade pbk.)
    1. Persuasion (Psychology) I. Title.

BF637.P4 M38 2002
650.1'3—dc21   2001058971

The author may be contacted at:
  Rick Maurer
  rick@beyondresistance.com
  703-525-7074

Credits
Developmental editor: **Leslie Stephen**
Copy editors: **Rebecca Taff, Deborah Costenbader**
Proofreaders: **Steve Carrell, Deborah Costenbader, Luke Torn**
Text Design/Production: **Hespenheide Design**
Jacket Design: **Hespenheide Design**

First printing: February 2002

Dedicated to the memory of
my parents, Ed and Edith Maurer.

They seldom spoke about integrity,
they simply lived it.

CONTENTS

INTRODUCTION
The Promise of a Better Way   11

PART I   OPPOSITION AND SUPPORT

1   *The Life or Death of an Idea*   19

2   *Why They Don't Want What You Want*   33

3   *The Art of Building Commitment*   47
Includes interview with Senator George Mitchell,
chair of the Northern Ireland peace process

PART II   PRINCIPLES OF ENGAGEMENT

4   *Know Your Intention*   63

5   *Consider the Context*   79

6   *Avoid Knee-Jerk Reactions*   93

7   *Pay Attention*   109
Includes interview with Alan Alda, actor and director

8   *Explore Deeply*   123
Includes interview with Lynne Jacobs,
therapist and psychoanalyst

9   *Find Ways to Connect*   139
Includes interview with Neil Rackham,
researcher and author on effective sales

PART III THE FINE POINTS OF INFLUENCE AND ENGAGEMENT

10 *Stay Calm to Stay Engaged* 153

11 *Ways to Avoid Resistance in the First Place* 169
Includes interview with Mariah Burton Nelson,
author of *The Unburdened Heart*

12 *What to Do When the Principles Aren't Enough* 187

A FINAL WORD
Taking These Ideas Home 195

Resources 207
Endnotes 210
Acknowledgments 215
About the Author 216
Index 217
Order Information 224

The Promise of a Better Way

Why are some people successful in getting their ideas accepted and others are not? And what happens when we get our way but in the process hurt our relationship with the person we have persuaded to go along?

Think about the ways you try to get what you want. What do you usually do to —

- **Get a good idea accepted?** You've got an idea that you believe could really help your organization, but the one person who needs to grant approval isn't interested. What would you do?
- **Influence a team?** You own a small five-person business. You need this team to act like owners, think strategically, and make quick decisions on their own. But everyone waits for you to decide things. You demand, you plead, you even bought motivational tapes for the gang, but nothing changes. What would you do?
- **Move into new technology?** Your company has relied on print catalogues for eighty years, but it's time to move to the Internet. You can save money and provide new product and pricing information quicker and easier. Unfortunately, people in your company love their old catalogue, and you can't get anyone interested in even seriously considering a change. What would you do?

12   *Introduction*

- **Change the focus of your mission?** You serve on the board of a local service group that is an institution in your community. The demographics of the town have changed over the past few years and the types of services you provide aren't needed as much. You believe that your service club should reconsider its mission. But whenever you bring this up, you are treated as if you are speaking heresy. What would you do?
- **Create a strategic alliance?** If your company formed a strategic alliance with a competitor, you could provide an unparalleled level of products and services to customers. But the leaders in the other company are suspicious of your company's intentions. You've as much as said, "It's OK, you can trust us," but you can feel the hostility when you meet with them. What would you do next?
- **Avoid change for change's sake?** After the merger, the new headquarters team has pushed to change most business practices to conform to the way the acquiring company does things. But when you suggest that your company had a pretty good way of tracking inventory and you think they should consider adopting this system, they smile as if a five-year-old had just said the cutest thing. What would you do?
- **Influence a loved one?** You believe it's time to move. The house is too small, mortgage rates are low, and it is a buyer's market. Your partner likes everything about the old place. What would you do?

Why are we influential with some people, but completely miss the mark with others? Why do people resist ideas that we think are absolutely brilliant? Why do budding agreements break down into winner-take-all contests? Are there better ways to build support for our ideas and reap benefits from them?

Most changes, new initiatives, projects, or inventions demand that others not only like the idea but get behind it. Often we need more than just lip-service compliance; we need full commitment. We need those people to help with the heavy lifting. Without their help, a great new idea may never get off the ground. Most sobering of all, some failed ideas can take the company down with them. The costs are so high and the need so great, that it may be difficult or impossible to recover from this lost opportunity.

Through sheer force, I may be able to muscle through a decision from you today, but then find that my actions have begun to damage our working relationship. Next time I come to you, you're wary and hold back. And, over time, I may completely destroy our relationship. Just look around for evidence of this. It's everywhere: at work, on sales calls, in civic and church groups, and at home. Undoubtedly, you've come into contact with someone at work whose ham-handed approach to change has alienated you to the extent that you don't even consider his or her ideas anymore. This person couldn't convince you to leave a burning building. And we all know of made-in-heaven marriages that end in a most human institution — the courts.

This book provides a way to meet our goals in ways that can actually strengthen relationships. This builds a foundation for the next time and the time after that. Instead of eroding the structures of the bridge between us, our strategies actually strengthen our capacity to get work done.

Many people say they want to meet their objectives in ways that serve the larger good. I believe people when they say this. I even believe it when I say it, but something happens that subverts those intentions. At the first sign of resistance, we may revert to some win-lose tactic that ends all conversation. Sticking with the other person can be difficult when tension between us is high. But, as I hope to demonstrate, staying connected is essential to get people excited about our ideas. In this book, my goal is to show you how to avoid those knee-jerk reactions that often make matters worse.

Many books on change and influence focus on making a compelling case for our cause. That's important, of course, but it's usually not sufficient. This book asks you to expand your thinking beyond the idea itself to include the relationship with the other person. Sometimes a person's reaction to you or to the idea may be more important than the idea itself.

Why Don't You Want What I Want? focuses on you and your relationship with some person or small group that you want to influence: a salesperson with a prospect, an executive with a vice-president, a project leader and his or her team, or a secretary and boss. The main focus is influencing others at work, but you probably will begin to see ways these ideas apply at home and in the community as well.

Even the largest changes in organizations often begin with one-on-one encounters. For example, if I can't convince the head of accounting that an idea is good, it will never get to the COO. As a union rep, if I can't make the production manager interested in my ideas, I'll be in for a fight. The ability to land a major account may hinge on your ability to convince a lone executive secretary to allow you into the CEO's inner sanctum. This book is an invitation to pay attention to these critical relationships.

For almost a decade, I have focused my work on resistance to change. The questions Why do people oppose us? and Why do people support us? are two sides of a single coin. This book explores why people offer their support — and why they resist us. I believe it is essential to understand both sides of that coin.

My search for answers to the challenge of resistance began in psychology, but soon expanded to management. In *Beyond the Wall of Resistance*, I explored some of the innovative management practices that were successful in building support for change among large groups of people. As I expanded my focus to include one-on-one relationships, my dormant background in theater came alive. I realized that the training actors receive is similar to what we need in order to stay open to other people while we hang onto our own objectives. I began combining what I had learned from psychology, management, theater, meditation, principled negotiation, and the philosophy of Martin Buber into a stew.

For the past few years, I've been using the ideas in this book with clients. People who have put them into practice tell me that they are now more influential — they get things done with fewer fights, headaches, power plays, counterpunches, and Machiavellian tactics. And they are able to get agreement while actually making the relationship with the other person stronger. So, instead of destroying bonds, their way of approaching others improves the chances that they'll have a receptive audience in the future.

Are these ideas the last word in an approach to influence that blends our intentions with the wishes and aspirations of the other person? No. I hope others will play with the ingredients in this stew. But I've seen these principles work effectively in large and small situations: from helping leaders build support for a reorganization, assisting managers to integrate two departments after a merger, getting support for a new software system, or even something as small as persuading a gatekeeper to let you have five minutes with a key decision maker.

There are some instances that go beyond the scope of this book. For instance, if you are in an abusive relationship at work or home, the last thing you need to hear is that there is something else you should be doing. Get out of harm's way, and don't keep thinking that it's all up to you. This book won't help you.

And if you view everything as a contest — you love the game itself, you like to keep score, and you especially like to come out on top over the other person — you'll hate this book.

But if you believe that there are instances at work or elsewhere in your life where you could refine the way you try to influence others to accept your thinking, please read on.

PART I

Opposition and Support

CHAPTER 1

The Life or Death of an Idea

What we know is what we accept. It's like that everywhere.
— Lorraine Hansberry, *Les Blancs*

Bill was CEO of a small company that manufactured and sold street lamps to cities. He was worried. What had once been a few glitches here and there in filling customer orders was beginning to look like a major problem. Customers were complaining. Orders were getting lost in the system. Specifications would mysteriously get changed as they passed from one department to another. He had to do something.

After thinking about this for some time, he decided to bring in a new software system that would change everything. A single system would allow each department to see what others were doing. No more garbled messages. No more wondering about the status of a customer's order. Once a salesperson entered the order into the system, everyone would work from the same set of data.

Bill talked with his senior team about this. They said they liked it. He hired consultants to get everything up and running. As he talked to employees about the proposed change, he heard a few grumbles, but most people, for the most part, seemed pleased. Some even said, "It's about time."

People got training. The new software was installed, and then the real problems began. Nothing worked like Bill had hoped it would. He poured more money into the project, but things didn't improve. He begged, he demanded, and he spent even more money to get things up and running. In the end, the costs and headaches far exceeded the few benefits his company gained from the new software.

You may know someone like Bill. You might even think you are the model for this story. In truth, Bill is a composite of many executives, managers, and project leaders I've known. These men and women were bright, committed to their organizations, saw a need, and tried to implement a solution, only to see the project die.

Of course there are all types of variations on this theme: why some people are able to turn good ideas into action and get the results they want, while others see idea after idea flounder and die.

- Why is one manager able to capture the interest of employees in a way that they are eager to do whatever it takes to make a new project a success, and another manager meets intense opposition every step of the way?
- How can a salesperson who knows her product well, and seems to know countless techniques for closing a sale, consistently do so poorly? How can another salesperson across town, who seems to use no particular technique to get people to buy, repeatedly make big sales?
- What's the difference between the person whose suggestions are ignored and the person who can present the very same idea and have others say, "That's a great idea. Let's do it."?

Often the difference between people who see ideas turn into action and their less-than-successful counterparts is subtle. It has to do with what they choose to pay attention to once they get an idea in their heads.

A LIMITED VIEW

In the movie version of *West Side Story*, Tony attends a dance at the gym. Across the room, he sees Maria. All else fades from view. He can see nothing but her. Our ideas can affect us like that. Once we get a vision in our head, all else goes out of focus. We miss the fact that Maria is a Shark and we are a Jet, and our respective gangs hate each other. We block out all the reasons why meeting Maria could be ill-timed and dangerous for her, us, our friends, and our families. All we can see is Maria. We begin to believe that our idea is worthy, so no matter what others might think, we are going to move across the gym floor right now (singing a song as we go). We want to be with Maria and we want to be with her now. That narrow focus is fine, of course, unless we are going to need the support of others — say the Jets and the Sharks — if we ever hope to see this fabled romance make it through even a single night.

> Without intending it, our excitement for our ideas may make enemies out of the very people we want to join us.

Tony and Maria may have had alternatives. Of course, it would have made for a very boring musical, but there are ways Tony and Maria could have met, fallen in love, and even married, without bloodshed. But to do that, Tony and Maria would have had to expand their focus to consider other things.

When our idea demands the support of others, we have no choice but to expand our view of the scene to include the Jets, the Sharks, the history of these two cultures in New York City, timing — and the list goes on. Without this expanded field of vision our chance to live happily ever after goes way down. When we focus on just our idea or goal or vision, we create two major challenges for ourselves.

Challenge # 1: When We Get Too Far Ahead

When we get caught up in our own idea, we can get way ahead of where others may be in thinking about how to solve a problem or seize an opportunity. For example, we have a feeling that something's not quite right — or we see an opportunity. The thought rumbles around in our brains, picking up momentum. We start to get ideas on ways to address this situation. As we think about it, we start to see solutions, then ways to implement our plan. Visions of budgets and timelines dance in our heads. We envision how good life will be after everyone implements the solution we've come up with. And we picture the adulation that will be ours once people hear about our brilliant idea.

When we announce the plan, it is well thought-out, complete with action steps. In the meantime, no one else has even been thinking about this issue. When we present our plan, people are stunned. The more we try to explain and sell our idea, the more opposition we encounter.

Our enthusiasm can be a good thing. It's called creativity, intuition, and leadership. But the challenge is staying excited about our idea and staying engaged with the person who needs to support us.

> The challenge is staying excited about our idea and staying engaged with the person who needs to support us.

When it comes time to implement the plan, there's no one there to help with the heavy lifting. We see whatever potential the idea had for increased revenues, greater efficiency, improved anything dwindle. And sometimes the recognition that we were really out there alone comes after a considerable amount of time, expense, and work has gone into pushing the idea.

When we are out ahead on an issue, we may miss the fact that others have been working on ideas too — and those ideas might complement ours or even compete with ours. It is even possible that what they are seeing may be even a better way to go.

Challenge # 2: When We Miss Their Reactions
The second challenge comes when our own excitement over our idea shuts down our ability (or willingness) to pay attention to the reactions of other people. Whether we intend it or not, we are showing that the other person's opinion doesn't matter. With most changes, though, there are people who must support us: people who must beat the drums, cough up dollars, and send people to training. And there are others whose support or opposition won't count for much. Too often, we fail to distinguish between the support we *must* have and the support that would be *nice* to have.

After Tony and Maria got together, both were given plenty of advice that they should slow down. But neither would hear a word of it; they were too much in love to listen to reason. When we ignore or fail to see in the first place, we are missing the signals that let us know whether people are excited or skeptical, pleased or angry. We miss the very signals that allow us to build support.

Every day, major projects and minor dreams are killed for no other reason than people get more excited about the idea than they do about what it will take to build support for it. Once we get ahead of others in our thinking and fail to take the reactions of others into account, we are not in a good position to influence them to want what we want.

A BETTER WAY

If you've worked in any organization for very long, it may be difficult to see how focusing on just the idea isn't enough. It may seem that virtually every meeting you go to, every hallway conversation, every e-mail focuses solely on ideas and the procedures to get them implemented. We may believe wrongly that the idea itself is the only thing to focus on. But there is a better way. Just consider these examples:

In a Hospital. Peggie was director of nursing in a major hospital in a state that allowed unlicensed personnel to perform some of the simpler nursing functions, like changing simple wound dressings. In an effort to control costs, the executive team of the hospital decided to add a number of unlicensed people to the payroll. Nurses saw this as a threat. Peggie knew that nurses would need to champion this change or else it would fail. They were the ones who would be working side by side with these untrained staff. Without guidance and informal supervision, the new employees would waste money rather than save it, and there was the possibility that they could put patients at risk.

Peggie believed that if she could talk directly to the nurses and explain why this was important, they would support this decision. She scheduled a series of small group meetings, so each nurse would have a chance to talk directly with Peggie. The first meeting went all right, but Peggie missed some of the unasked questions. During subsequent meetings, she picked up on the unasked questions, and addressed the impact this decision could have on patient care as well as job security for nurses. She truly believed that this decision would improve patient care because nurses would have more time to focus on more critical needs. And she believed that this decision was necessary for the survival of the institution. In each of these meetings, many nurses changed their positions and a fair number even volunteered to work with her to make sure the transition went smoothly.

In a Bank. James was a new officer in a major bank who was given the task of coordinating the work with federal regulators. Bankers and regulators often have an arm's length adversarial relationship. Neither side trusts the other much. Consequently, regulators can make life miserable for people like James. They can demand lots of time, generate paperwork, and cause headaches. On the other side of this coin, bank employees had gotten used to stonewalling requests and in general playing a passive-aggressive game with the regulators.

Assuming that the regulators probably entered these relationships with similar concerns, James set up a meeting with the regulators. But before the two teams got together, he called his regulator counterpart to tell him what he had planned for this unusual meeting. The next morning, some forty people got together. James said, "You need us and we need you. You've got an important job to do and, frankly, we need to be able to demonstrate that you're watching over us." He suggested that they cooperate. The regulators and his own team were highly and vocally skeptical, but were willing to give it a try.

He initiated two types of recurring weekly meetings: one to discuss day-to-day tactical issues, another to discuss overall management and how they were working together. This decision saved James and his team countless hours of strained meetings and urgent paperwork requests. James has moved on, but the system is still in place and working well for both sides some five years later.

In a School System. Pat is superintendent of a school system that was engaged in months-long contract negotiations with the local teachers' union. Things escalated from mild discontent to acrimonious tension. The chance of a settlement seemed to slip further from grasp.

The negotiating teams were deadlocked. Pat believed that if she and the union president, Frederick, could reach an agreement between themselves, they could remove the roadblock. She invited him to meet with her privately and off the record. Pat said, "Frederick, you and I both need to get this settled. I know the pressure you're under." He agreed. Pat told him that this situation was no easier for her. And she assured him that she would not tell anyone about the meeting. They met, exchanged private cell phone numbers so they could keep in touch, and continued to meet for the next two months.

This image appears throughout the book with notes that link the content of that chapter to the key lenses of

○ understanding/
misunderstanding
○ favorable reactions/
unfavorable reactions
○ trust/mistrust

When they finally did work out an agreement, Pat and Frederick presented their ideas to their respective teams. Both liked what they heard. The proposed contract was put to a vote of members and ratified.

THE WAY TO A BETTER WAY

Peggie, James, and Pat have something in common: All three realized that people — sometimes it was just one other person — were critical to building support for their ideas. It was as if all three knew that their success rested on three pillars: under-standing, favorable reactions, and trust.

Understanding
Of course, focusing on what you want — the idea itself — is important. But even though we may be geniuses at developing our arguments, making presentations, pointing out the logical reasons why this is such a good idea, we may still miss looking through the lens of understanding. Do they get it? Do they understand what we are saying?

Understanding is not the same as agreement. With understanding, all we need is for people to say, "I get it" or "I see what you mean." Our enthusiasm to keep pushing our idea ahead can inhibit our ability to know if they do get it. We mix up why and how.

Here's what goes wrong. We have started explaining *how* our idea needs to be implemented, but people are still wondering *why* this thing is even worth considering. They don't understand our reasoning. They don't see why we believe this idea is important right now. Mixing why and how is dangerous. We can't expect others to understand instantly what took us weeks or months to see. People need time to see the same picture we see. When we rush the process, we fail to give others time to see the same picture we've just developed.

In Peggie's work with the nurses, she felt it was critical that the nurses fully understand the implications of the decision to hire non-licensed personnel. They needed to know what was involved, when the hiring would begin, how many would be hired, and they needed to understand that if they didn't do this, the hospital's cost of doing business could make it uncompetitive in their city.

> When trying to influence someone, separate *why* you believe the idea is important from *how* you want to implement it.

Pat needed Frederick to fully grasp what was most important from where she sat. She could not accept any contract offer that failed to place a cap on spending. It was also important for her to find out what was most critical for Frederick.

Reaction

You can't take support for granted. Just because you love your own idea doesn't guarantee that others will. The fact is, people may hate the idea. The reaction lens helps us see how people are responding. We need to know just how receptive they are likely to be. There are five major reactions you could get when you present your idea to someone else:

1. Champion. The champion is so excited about your idea that he or she is willing to do whatever it takes to ensure the idea gets implemented in a way that gets results. The champion might offer to lead, go to bat for you with someone else, or protect your time so you can keep this idea a top priority.

2. Support. The supporter likes your idea and is quite willing to help you whenever you ask. He won't take a leadership role but will be glad to assist if asked.

3. Go Along. This person will go along with your idea. She won't take any initiative, but she won't make waves either. Don't expect someone at this stage to volunteer for a task force, commit resources, or do anything to further the cause. She will simply go along.

4. Drag Feet. This person doesn't like the idea. Perhaps he doesn't understand it fully, so for now he is uncomfortable with your idea. Or perhaps he grasps what you are suggesting but simply doesn't like it. If you ask him to do something, he will probably complain or find ways to proceed by exerting only minimal effort. Or, as a client once described it, he will use malicious compliance.

5. Actively Oppose. This person really truly doesn't like your idea and will do whatever he or she can to make sure your idea never succeeds.

For someone to support or champion an idea, there must be an emotional reaction in favor of the idea. Something needs to hit them in a way that they not only see the potential value but feel its importance. Without this emotional charge, the best you can expect is that people might go along, but you run the risk of getting foot dragging or active opposition.

People who are at the champion or support stage are leaning in favor of you and your idea. People who are dragging their feet or actively opposing you may demand your time, energy, and attention since they are working against you. And, their work is easier. It is far easier to stop a project than to get one started.

Getting a favorable reaction goes beyond just providing information. Understanding is necessary, but not sufficient. In addition to understanding, you will most likely need others to react favorably. This reaction is emotional. It is the world of excitement, anticipation, hope, and optimism.

James had been around the block, and so had the regulators. Unless he did something, both sides would drag their feet or actively oppose the other group. His strategy was an attempt to

STAGES OF AN IDEA

Knowing where you are in your thinking and where other people are can begin to show you where and how to engage others. You can only do this if you pay attention to the signals. Your desire to get things accomplished may get in the way of keeping your eyes open to what's going on around you.

Stage 1: Scanning the Horizon Looking at Possibilities
Small things. You see a glimmer of a potential problem or opportunity. No thoughts are well formed yet. You are just looking.

Implications: This is the best place to get others involved. You're still in the exploration stage, just keeping your eyes open to potential opportunities and threats.

Stage 2: Recognizing That Something Must Be Done
In cartoons, this is where the light bulb goes on above someone's head. This is the stage where you recognize a problem or an opportunity. You still don't know what to do about it, but you know that something needs to happen.

Implications: This is still a good place to get support. You have an opportunity to show others what you are seeing. Even if trust is low, the fact that you're not suggesting any action yet may keep resistance lower than it would be if you were about to launch a new program.

Stage 3: Beginning to Move Ahead
You're moving from recognition of the problem to doing something about it. Once you move to action, it gets harder to get others to support you. In effect, you're saying, "Here's the problem, and I've made up my mind what we're going to do about it."

Implications: Moving to action can imply that you believe your way of connecting dots is the right way and those of us who don't see things your way must be a bit slow. People don't like that. If you're at the moving-ahead stage, be careful. You're moving away from a place where you can be influenced easily.

Stage 4: Ready to Implement
You're ready to dig the foundation, book passage on the ship, roll out the plan, get this thing up and running.

Implications: At this stage, you leave little room for others to influence your decision. While there will be times when you may want to make unilateral decisions, I assume you're reading this book because you want to stay excited about your idea and stay engaged with other people.

turn potentially negative reactions into positive ones. Peggie's success came when she addressed the unasked questions. In one of the meetings, she said, "If I were in your shoes, I'd be worried about my job — and I'd be worried about the risk this might pose to my own nursing license." With that statement, she hit two of the major concerns that would cause nurses to resist this change. When she addressed the third major concern — quality of patient care — and asked for their help in ensuring that it remained high, many were on her side.

When you need supporters and champions you need people who

- don't just recognize but can feel the potential benefits of this idea,
- are optimistic when they envision the outcome,
- believe you have their best interests in mind (and at heart) — and have confidence in your leadership.

Ask yourself, would you support or champion a new idea or a major change in your organization that didn't meet those simple criteria? Probably not. But every day, people try to sell us on their ideas without taking time to address these issues — or even noticing whether we are reacting favorably.

Trust

Understanding what you have in mind and having a favorable reaction are important, but that still may not be enough. The quality of your relationship also matters. Do people trust you and your judgment? Do they think you are the person to do the job? If so, they may already be inclined to give you the benefit of any doubt and react favorably. If not, all the selling points in the world probably won't help you make your case.

As you'll see in the next chapter, our relationship with the other person can be formed by many factors — some of which are out of our control. For instance, I am a consultant. When I work outside the United States, I have two things going against me: first, I am a consultant and, second, I am an American. There is a tendency for people in corporations around the world to think that American consultants are arrogant know-it-alls, who believe they have nothing to learn from anyone else and are always trying to sell you something.

APPLY THE 5/5 TEST

How much support do you really need for your idea? This simple tool can help you answer that question.

A. Identify someone you need to talk with about one of your ideas.
B. Rate him/her on a scale from 1 to 5.
> 5 = You need them to be an active champion for the idea.
> 4 = You need them to support the idea.
> 3 = You need them to go along with the idea.
> 2 = It is OK if they drag their feet.
> 1 = It is OK if they actively oppose this idea.

C. Now rate him/her again on a scale of 1 to 5. This time focus on the level of support you are likely to get.
> 5 = It is likely that they will actively champion your idea.
> 4 = They will probably support your idea.
> 3 = They will probably go along.
> 2 = They are likely to drag their feet.
> 1 = They are likely to oppose you actively.

D. If you are going to be successful, the numbers should match. If you need a 5, you should expect to get a 5. If you only need a 3, the other person should be at 3 (or higher). Mismatches are dangerous. If you need a 5 and only expect a 2 or 3, pay particular attention to the challenges here and to the principles described in the following chapters. I will argue that the principles in this book can be applied in most any situation where we want to influence others. However, I believe they are absolutely essential when we need a 5 and are likely to get something lower.

Sadly, much of this perception is based on their own experience working with American consultants.

These suspicions exist before they ever meet me. Some in the group may know nothing about me, but they do know consultants — and they don't trust them. Is that unfair? Yes, but that's life and I had better recognize that fact. If I ignore the strong possibility that they are going to be wary of me and I just stride in touting my ideas, they're not likely to hear what I say. What they will hear will be filtered through their beliefs about what I must be like. Unless I find a way to demonstrate I am different in some significant ways, I am likely to fail.

Better salespeople understand that building a solid relationship counts for more than any set of sales techniques. This same thing applies in politics. In surveys, people tend to like the member of Congress who represents them, but they tend to distrust Congress. Former U.S. Speaker of the House Tip O'Neill had it right when he said that all politics are local. He understood that it is the personal relationships and connections that matter most.

Both Pat and Peggie enjoyed some trust going into their conversations. James was an unknown, but the regulators did know other bank executives so they were likely to be skeptical of him. When James talked with them candidly about what relationships had looked like in the past, they began to feel like just maybe this guy was different.

SEEING THE FULL PICTURE

I believe that we need to pay equal attention to understanding (Do they get it?), to reactions (Do they like it?), and to trust (Are they going to be receptive to me and what I have to say?). Often people try to influence others in ways that ignore all of these considerations. This book focuses on ways to increase our skill in gaining understanding, encouraging favorable reactions, and building trust.

The opposites of understanding, favorable reactions, and trust are the seeds of most resistance to our ideas. Recognizing why resistance occurs is a critical skill in knowing how to build support for our ideas. And that leads us to the next chapter.

CHAPTER 2

Why They Don't Want What You Want

In all matters of opinion our adversaries are insane.

— Oscar Wilde

If people understand our idea, react favorably to it, and trust us, it is likely that they just might want what we want. It looks so simple and easy on paper, doesn't it? Unfortunately, getting understanding, sparking favorable reactions, and ensuring sufficient trust is challenging. Each of these conditions has another side. And it's that side that is the breeding ground for resistance.

Studies in organizations show that resistance is the primary reason why all manner of major changes fail. If we only focus on what we want, we fail to grasp the power and importance of resistance. Resistance is the one-word reason why they don't want what we want. Understanding resistance can help in two fundamental ways. First, if we understand what causes resistance, we often can avoid it before it occurs. Second, during those times when the train is already about to derail, understanding resistance can help us get things back on track.

Think of lack of understanding, unfavorable reactions, and mistrust as three levels of resistance, each one more challenging than the last. At its simplest, they either understand the idea or they don't (Level 1). They either react positively or negatively (Level 2). They either trust us or they don't (Level 3).

Of course, all three of these levels are in play all the time, sometimes working in our favor, sometimes working against us. Ideally, the person we want to influence gets what the idea is about, sees some benefit in it for her, and trusts what we say. Resistance occurs when one or more of the levels is working against us: Someone might trust our judgment, understand what we are saying, but something about the idea scares him. Or even worse, someone might not understand our idea, strongly dislike what they hear, and believe that we're the wrong person to lead this endeavor.

LEVEL 1: LACK OF UNDERSTANDING

Level 1 resistance is based on the content of the idea. Others simply may need more information or be confused by what we are telling them. Perhaps they just need time to *think* about the proposition. Level 1 resistance involves the world of thinking and rational action. This is the world of facts, figures, and data. Level 1 lends itself to explanation and answering people's questions. The goal in working with Level 1 resistance is to increase understanding.

Level 1 resistance may also come from a disagreement over interpretation of the data. Imagine that one person in an office is a champion of one word processing program, and another loves what a competitor offers. Each person's resistance to the other's favorite is based on his or her interpretation of what is important. For example, one person may place more value on the word processor's capacity to design newsletters, while another cares most about the ease of typing straightforward documents. Each interprets the data based on his or her own interests. No power struggles, nothing under the table — these people simply disagree about the importance of what each software package offers. Mathematicians who worked for years on the perplexing Fermat's Theorem seemed to take delight when a colleague found another way into the puzzle, even when it disagreed with their own work.[1] Even though some of these mathematicians had devoted their lives to this quest, the search for mathematical truth was more important than ego.

Most of our tools for working with resistance in organizations are designed to assist us with Level 1 issues: PowerPoint® and similar presentation software, newsletters, videos, question-and-answer sessions, and debate all work well when the issue is confined to the mostly rational domain. But, as you'll see, the resistance that keeps us up at night is seldom Level 1.

Another variation of Level 1: Sometimes people need to see or experience something in order for them to understand it. Les Paul, a pioneer of the electric guitar, brought his new invention to a gig. Because it was electronic, it didn't need the large hollow sound chamber of an acoustic

LEVEL 1 RESISTANCE

I don't *get* it.

guitar. It was ugly and looked nothing like a traditional guitar. Basically, it was a four-by-four hunk of wood with strings and amp pickups attached. People said it looked like a log. "It was funny, you know: I went and played a gig in Long Island, and we got such a bad reaction you can't believe it . . . it was the dog of dogs," Mr. Paul remembered.[2] He came back with a traditional-looking guitar that had all the electronic stuff hidden inside. People loved it. This simple gesture — manipulative in a most positive sense of the word — allowed people to hear his music instead of being blocked by what they assumed a log must sound like.

Recent brain research indicates that there may not be the separation between thoughts and emotions that was so commonly believed. In other words, to even become interested or excited in something suggests that our emotions are involved in some way. Even with our slideshow presentations, we need to accept the fact that life is more than bullet points and graphs. People need our help in getting interested in our ideas. For instance, car salespeople give test drives. The drive can help answer Level 1 questions — such as "How does the car handle?" — but it can also give you the feel of the car, and that takes you out of the purely rational into an emotional experience.

The fact that many decisions mix rational and emotional elements is not a problem. The problem comes when we assume that we are making purely rational decisions. Take investing, for example. William Goetzmann, finance professor at Yale, suggests that "investors typically prize investments they already own and tend to ignore information that suggests they made a bad choice." He says that "even relatively sophisticated investors not only overestimate the returns of their funds, but they also overestimate the returns relative to a benchmark."[3]

When we are attempting to get someone interested in our ideas, it is helpful to realize that their response to what we say often includes elements of understanding, emotional reactions, and trust — in other words, their response is grounded in all three levels of potential resistance.

LEVEL 2: NEGATIVE EMOTIONAL REACTIONS

Level 2 resistance is emotional. Our bodies react. Our heart rate increases, pumping more blood to the large muscles. Adrenaline rushes through our bodies. We are getting ready for what typically is called *fight or flight*.

We are exhibiting what neuroscientist Joseph LeDoux calls "the fear response."[4] LeDoux says that the emotions, not the intellect, are the most basic survival mechanism of all living organisms. Our emotions warn us of danger and allow us to take action instantly, before our conscious mind even knows what's going on. Imagine that you hear a loud crash as you read this sentence. You probably would cover your head and crouch instantly, and only then would you look up to see where the sound came from. You would have taken those protective actions without your conscious mind considering what to do. If the ceiling had been caving in, there would not have been time for thoughtful consideration. Your rapid instinctive reaction could have saved your life.

Charles Darwin once entered the snake house at the London Zoo and stood before a puff adder, a highly venomous snake. The puff adder struck and Darwin recoiled. He was surprised by his response, since a glass partition separated him from the snake. Darwin then tried an experiment. He stood in front of the snake and tried to keep from moving when it struck. But each time, Darwin flinched. Even though he knew there was no danger, his need for self-protection was so strong that it overrode his conscious desire to stand firm.[5]

LEVEL 2 RESISTANCE

I don't *like* it.

These instinctive reactions, designed to protect people, occur whether a snake is lunging at our faces or a potentially threatening idea comes at us. In addition to fight or flight, we may become immobilized like a deer caught in the headlights or submit much like an animal does when it rolls on its back and exposes its vital organs.[6] In a study at UCLA, researchers found that there seems to be a gender difference in how we handle stress. Women more typically "tend and befriend." The research did not focus specifically on the fear response, but it is worth noting that there may be a wider range of options than just fight, flight, or immobilize that occur in that first split second when the puff adder strikes.[7]

In chapter 1, I identified five possible reactions people might have to our ideas: They could champion, support, go along, drag their feet, or actively oppose us. Sometimes our ideas may trigger a fear response that causes the other person to drag his or her feet or actively oppose us. In other words, we become the puff adder and cause this resistance.

The Power of Fear

Level 2 resistance is almost always grounded in a fear of something related to the idea. Here is a partial list of some of these fear responses:

- Fear that one will lose face. Something about this idea will make the person look bad in front of others.
- Fear that one will lose status. This idea will reduce the person's status in the family or organization.
- Fear that this idea will cost the person her job or endanger financial security.
- Fear of failure. If the person's image of himself is based on winning, then failure is not an option for him.
- Fear of loss of life or being physically hurt in some way.
- Fear that an idea will harm those one loves.
- Fear that one will lose control over something important.

People sometimes dismiss emotions as soft and touchy-feely. That's almost always a mistake. When people are afraid they will lose something important — when their fear response kicks in — their emotional brain takes over and limits their ability to stay engaged with us.

Level 2 Hinders Communication

According to John Gottman's research on couples, when our resting pulse rate increases by a mere 10 percent, our ability to communicate decreases.[8] Gottman found that when the pulse rate goes up to 100, communication becomes terribly strained. In other words, it is very difficult to continue working on Level 2 issues when our hearts start beating faster.

Level 2 Can Fester
In the rest of the animal kingdom, these emergency reactions come and go. A mouse sees a cat. In a split second, the mouse reacts and gets out of harm's way. Once the Fluffy the Cat crisis passes, the mouse's system goes back to normal. Humans are different. We hang onto things. We worry, we stew in our own juices, we fantasize, we speculate. When we stay in Level 2 for too long, we may begin to hold tension in our muscles, always vigilant in case someone attacks us. Our digestive systems run riot. Our nights are sleepless.

I tell you about my idea to move the business in a different direction. This frightens you. You fear that you won't be needed and you could lose your job. You can't eat or sleep. When I speak or send you an e-mail, you examine everything for signs that this fear could be realized. You are on constant fight-flight alert.

Mr. Einstein, Meet Mr. Neanderthal
LeDoux's recent research shows that some stimuli actually bypass the cognitive domains of the brain. In other words, the emotional system can operate on its own, without involving any conscious, cognitive function. That's the reason why Darwin could not stop himself from flinching. The portion of the brain called the amygdala can "make up its own mind" in a split second, causing you to pull back from the snake no matter what the higher centers of the brain tell you about the real risk.

Imagine a salesperson trying to sell a new bells-and-whistles copier to a client. He talks about features and benefits, but the client is worried that he will look bad if this purchase seems like a waste of money. As the salesperson continues his well-reasoned Level 1 presentation, the potential customer is literally responding from a different place. The salesperson is speaking from the neocortex, the customer is responding from the amygdala. Mr. Einstein, meet Mr. Neanderthal. (And, of course, this phenomenon applies to Ms. Einstein and Ms. Neanderthal as well.) The salesperson's approach is about 100,000 years too advanced for his intended audience at this moment. The more primitive portion of our distant ancestral brain is getting ready for fight or flight.

Margaret tried explaining repeatedly to her elderly father that due to his failing eyesight, it was no longer safe for him to drive. She was calm, rational, and gave him the facts. She even gave examples of times he had put himself and others at risk. She spoke out of a deep concern for his well-being. What she failed to realize was that her fine Level 1 arguments pushed her father into Level 2. For her father, this was a highly charged emotional issue. Losing the ability to drive meant he would lose independence and control. That scared him — his self-esteem was wrapped up in being able to live without being dependent on anyone else. He balked, refusing to listen or talk about this issue. He refused to give her his keys. He insisted he was competent and accused her of not trusting him. The next time she brought up driving, he changed the subject.

Margaret's story is not about who is right and who is wrong; it is about a failure to communicate at the appropriate level. She was speaking the language of Level 1 — sound, rational information. Her father heard the words, but they elicited a Level 2 reaction. Refusing to relinquish his keys was his equivalent of the fight response. When he changed the subject, he was engaging in a socially acceptable version of flight.

Imagine an executive talking to one of her middle managers about the state of their business. She makes a convincing case that shows the potential crisis that they could face if business doesn't pick up soon. She makes sound projections and analyses of financial performance. Her conversation is clear, Level 1 stuff. And then, almost as an afterthought, she happens to say that they might need to consider downsizing later on. To the manager, that single word stands out from all the rest. He doesn't hear the words "sometime later" or "a remote possibility"; he hears only "downsizing." The fear response kicks in, warning him that he is at risk. The executive may as well stop trying to persuade with Level 1 arguments, because her audience of one is listening to the Level 2 messages that are running riot inside his own mind.

LEVEL 3: LACK OF TRUST

In Level 1 and Level 2 resistance, the person is reacting to something about the idea itself. Level 3 resistance is bigger than that. People may not be resisting the idea — in fact they may love it. They are resisting *you*. Level 3 is the domain of deeply entrenched beliefs, experiences, and biases.

Level 3 resistance is often bigger than us, but since we are the ones trying to get our ideas across, we become the focal point. We may assume that since we are nice people and have the best interests of the organization at heart, none of these deeper issues should really matter. Failure to treat Level 3 as real and legitimate is a significant reason why many ideas fail.

The brain works by putting things into categories. This helps us get through life, but it also limits what we see and how we judge our world and the people in it.[9] Imagine seeing the world through green-tinted glasses. Everything is a shade of green. When someone points out some pretty yellow birds, you only see green finches. Green plants are green, but so are all the other plants.

LEVEL 3 RESISTANCE

I don't *trust* you.

In all Level 3 issues, we tend to see only those things that support our current way of looking at the world. We miss the yellows, reds, and blues. In some instances we acquire these glasses through life's experiences; in others, we are given them at birth.

Here is a description of the most common ways in which Level 3 resistance occurs.

History Together

John Gottman describes couples whose history together causes them to become flooded with emotion. Each exchange may carry the weight of years of being together.[10] Being late for an agreed-on appointment, or even forgetting to take the trash out, can cause one or both people to fall into Level 3 responses. Everything is bigger than the event at hand. This is the realm of "You always do this" and "You never do that."

When flooded with emotion, people become so overwhelmed by the circumstances that they cannot separate the current situation from their history together. Jeff and Paula have been married for ten years. Five years ago, Jeff had an affair. Although he soon realized that the affair was a mistake and ended that relationship, the damage had been done. Paula found it hard to trust him anymore. Everything he said and did came to her filtered through the lens of his infidelity. Even when she wanted to trust him, she couldn't.

Watch *The Honeymooners* for an example of Level 3 in full flower, both sides making stronger and stronger statements based on raw emotion — or raw fear. Their exchanges usually end with Ralph saying, "One of these days, Alice, right to the moon!" If our lives were as neatly scripted as a sitcom, we'd make up in twenty-two minutes with, "Alice, you're the greatest." Unfortunately, real life isn't so tidy, and Level 3 issues linger and fester. There is emotional residue. The next argument (even the next conversation) is entered with caution.

Congressman John Lewis offers a key to unlocking Level 3 resistance. When Lewis was a Civil Rights activist in the 1960s, Governor George Wallace was a major force against this cause. "When I met George Wallace, I had to forgive him, because to do otherwise — to hate him — would only perpetuate the evil system we sought to destroy."[11] Forgiveness is extremely difficult, but it is one way to open the door to influence, especially in highly polarized Level 3 situations.

Have you ever been burned by someone at work? You thought you could trust this person and then he did something that undermined you. Now you take nothing he says at face value. Everything that person says sounds suspicious. You turn life into a Shakespearean tragedy, thinking that there must be a sinister motive behind all actions. That's the world of Level 3.

Whom You Represent

For some, past history is not limited to direct experiences with you. When union workers say, "You can't trust management," they usually are speaking from Level 3. Although this statement may come from actual experience with some managers, it is now extended to all management. If you are the manager in question, union workers' response to you may have little to do with you and a lot to do with the group you represent. (Of course, management can and does paint union workers with the same broad-brush strokes.)

Studies that ask participants to ascribe personality based on physical characteristics show sobering results. A mere glance at someone else gives us information about that person — and this information could be false. Unfortunately, we make these instantaneous decisions unconsciously, so we often are unaware of these assumptions and biases.[12]

Cultural Background

Our culture gives us tinted lenses as well. Since our culture surrounds us, it is hard to even imagine another reasonable way of looking at the world — green is the only color we've ever known. When our cultural bias is Level 3, we simply have no interest in even considering lifting our glasses to see whether there might be another color scheme out there.

Any statement that begins with "All people of this race (or color or culture or sexual orientation) are . . ." is a sign of this Level 3 worldview. Ethnic Albanians and Serbians in Yugoslavia, Palestinians and Israelis in the Middle East, Protestants and Catholics in Northern Ireland, relations between African-Americans and whites in the United States are all Level 3 cultural issues.

Strong Value Differences

When there are strong value differences, people oppose everything you and your idea stand for. In these situations, people

QUICK REMINDER

Consider spending some time developing your skill at recognizing the three levels of resistance. As you read the newspaper, look at disagreements between individuals as well as between countries and consider what levels of resistance are at play. As you sit in a meeting and watch others work together, or listen to comments and questions after a colleague's sales presentation, or overhear grumbling at the coffee machine, or watch as your children's play turns into a fight, begin to identify the levels that seem to be at work. This ability to distinguish Level 1 from Level 2 from Level 3 will serve you well as you begin to apply the principles of engagement. It is far easier to learn to identify the complexity of the resistance when you are not a player in the game.

tend to polarize. At its worst, each side believes it stands for all that is good, right, and fair. And they may believe that the other side is pure evil. Abortion is a Level 3 issue. Advocates who are pro-choice (giving a woman the right to choose whether or not to have an abortion) or pro-life (those who oppose abortion) are similar in at least one way: They both share deeply felt values regarding this issue. Their positions differ dramatically, but both sides strongly believe in their positions.

Among those who were against the U.S. war in Vietnam, there were many who assumed that people who supported the war could not be trusted. Not only did they disagree about the war, but they believed there was something fundamentally wrong with people who supported it. Of course, among those who supported the war, there were many who saw protesters as anti-Americans who shouldn't be listened to on any subject.

THE CHALLENGES OF WORKING AT LEVELS 2 AND 3

Although issues arising from Level 3 resistance are extremely difficult to resolve, the approaches to dealing with Level 2 and Level 3 are similar. Both types of resistance are emotional and cloud our ability to stay present and respond to the other person. If we want to meet our goals and maintain our relationships with those who oppose us, we must address this tougher emotional side. We must use strategies that allow us to stay in contact with the other person while keeping sight of our own goals and aspirations.

Conversation, Not Presentation
When resistance is Level 2 or 3, we may need to give up Level 1 explanations and presentations temporarily. What is needed is conversation. Give and take. Listening. We must find out what's going on or why they oppose this idea. Without that information, it is impossible to develop a strategy that addresses their concerns sufficiently for them to support us. For instance, if your proposal evokes a Level 2 fear that this will end my chances of ever getting funding for my own pet project, I will not be listening to your well-reasoned arguments. Most of my attention will be drawn to my own

personal and emotional response to the idea. You'll never know about these concerns unless you encourage conversation that gets at my reactions.

A warning: In highly charged political environments in which people speak cautiously, it can be difficult to get at Level 2 or Level 3 concerns. People know that it is usually safe to raise Level 1 issues, such as questions about the budget or timelines, but it is far riskier to mention a personal fear or to dare address a lack of trust between you and someone else — like your boss, for example. When people are reluctant to speak candidly about their emotional reactions or the trust and confidence they have in you, conversation — give-and-take — is an especially important method to get at these deeper issues.

When Both Sides Drop to Level 2

When we are excited about the prospects of some new idea, we don't want people to oppose us. At our best, we may be willing to entertain a few Level 1 questions about the details of our plan. As we prepare for a meeting, our attention may be focused on how we would respond to these information-based challenges. We give little thought to potential Level 2 concerns because we don't believe anyone could seriously object to this idea. So if people do object, we are startled. We respond with Level 1 data, but they are asking for something else. As the situation escalates, we find ourselves dropping into Level 2. Instead of addressing their fears, we react emotionally out of our own fear. The corporate puff adder strikes and we react emotionally, often with a fight or flight response.

Our own reactions when someone opposes our idea can be a significant challenge in themselves. My friend Richard once referred to meetings with his boss as "acid bath time." His boss tended to make work issues personal, and his caustic style of speaking made it difficult for Richard to keep calm when he tried to influence his boss. Sometimes just the thought of meeting with his boss sent Richard to Level 2. So when he did meet with his boss, his own emotional reaction made it difficult for him to stay calm long enough to make clear, rational points or to influence the direction of a discussion.

When both of you drop to Level 2, then you've got Neanderthal versus Neanderthal. Sort of like a World Federation of Wrestling grudge match. Neither side is in much of a frame of mind to explore options. You may find yourself reacting in an

EXPANDING THE FRAME
Levels of Resistance and Support

Each of the potential levels of support can also be a level of resistance as well. Whatever the issue, each level is present at all times.

Consider someone whom you want to influence. A quick mental check might give you valuable information about where you need to focus your attention.

Level 1

Resistance	*Support*
He/she doesn't understand the details, is confused, or disagrees with the conclusions I've drawn about the way I think we should go.	He/she understands the idea and its implications and agrees with me regarding its importance.

Level 2

Resistance	*Support*
He/she is afraid of the impact this idea might have on him/her or on people close to him/her. Something about the idea is threatening.	He/she is excited about the possibilities inherent in the idea. He/she sees potential benefit for him/herself or others he/she cares about.

Level 3

Resistance	*Support*
He/she doesn't trust me and is suspicious of what I might do. This may be based on our history together or on associations he/she makes due to some group I am part of.	He/she likes and respects me (or is inclined to respect me based on whom I represent). Even though he/she may not agree with me in the end, this person is likely to take my ideas seriously.

uncensored fashion. If you lean toward a fight response, you might say things like, "Oh, yeah? Over my dead body!" or "I dare you to say that again." If you are prone to use flight as your survival method of choice, you might think, "If he does that again, I'm leaving." Or perhaps you're like the child who puts fingers in his ears and chants, "I can't hear you. I can't hear you." All of these approaches, which I call knee-jerk reactions, inhibit our ability to influence someone else.

CHEER UP, RESISTANCE ISN'T ALL BAD

People resist us for good reasons. Take something as simple as Level 1 understanding. If they don't understand our idea, it makes sense that they won't get behind it. Why should they? And if our idea threatens them (Level 2), there is absolutely no reason why they should support us. And if they believe we represent all that is bad and wrong in the organization (Level 3), they would be foolish to jump on our bandwagon. Although it may feel like it at times, there are no born resisters — people just lying in wait to mess up our plans. People resist due to lack of understanding, negative reaction to the idea, or lack of trust between us.

So why is this good news? If we can figure out the real reasons why people oppose us or our ideas, we have a far greater chance of turning that resistance into support. I can't influence what I don't see.

Staying in synch with others is the most reliable way to build support for our ideas in ways that diminish the chances that resistance will take over. We need to continually remind ourselves to ask three essential questions:

1. Do they understand?
2. Are they reacting positively or negatively to my idea?
3. Is there sufficient trust between us for them to support me?

Keeping the three levels of resistance in mind can be challenging. The next chapter begins the exploration of principles that can help us keep understanding, reactions, and trust in mind as we work with others.

CHAPTER 3

The Art of Building Commitment

If it's worth doing, it's worth doing slowly.

— Mae West

When Bryan McGraw was thrust into a new role as quality officer at a military base, he faced lots of resistance. One key to his success was a chief master sergeant who was against quality improvement. Before Bryan took over this position, his predecessors had a contentious relationship with the top enlisted man. The sergeant resisted passively at first, but then began to push back with nasty memos and heated arguments. Due to his position and personal power, he was able to influence others to join in the resistance to quality improvement. Bryan had a problem.

He was told to ignore the sergeant. Someone advised, "He's a pothole. Drive around him." Bryan didn't take that advice. The chief master sergeant was an influential person and well respected. Bryan realized that the sergeant was a critical player. He made an effort to get to know him. "We found things we both enjoyed together. We were both passionate hockey fans." Over about a six-month period, he saw the relationship change. The sergeant started to become a supporter of quality.

Bryan said, "I started slipping in messages and asking questions. I began identifying things he was good at and showed how these linked to quality initiatives — picking potential winning battles and commenting, 'Oh, by the way, what you did was an example of quality improvement.' And I went out of my way to recognize the positive things he did."

Perhaps the greatest compliment came when the sergeant was retiring from service. He told Bryan, "I wish others had made the attempt and made me understand quality the way you did." He went on to say that Bryan's predecessors tried to train him, but they had never made an investment in him.

But the influence wasn't just one-way. I asked whether the sergeant had influenced him in any way. Bryan said, "I could float things by him and get his input. If he was critical of my ideas, that made me think and refocus."

Sometimes it takes the Bryans of the world to help us see that there are alternatives to pitfalls like "He's a pothole. Drive around him." Bryan avoided the serious consequences of the levels of resistance by first increasing trust, and then understanding and favorable reactions. His approach was to pay attention to what was important to him *and* to what the sergeant wanted. Sometimes this approach can be played out with the simple elegance that Bryan demonstrated; at other times it can be more complex, with the outcome not always certain.

Staying excited about an idea while staying engaged with the other person is a fundamentally different way of trying to influence others than we commonly see in our organizations and communities. Staying excited about our ideas and staying engaged is not a simple tactic that we resort to when all else fails. It is a way of meeting the other person, whether things are going well or things are going poorly. It is a way of using the lenses of understanding, reactions, and trust in ways that often can avoid most of the harmful resistance. Paying attention to understanding, reactions, and trust increases our chances of getting people interested in our ideas.

> Staying excited about our ideas and staying engaged is not a simple tactic that we resort to when all else fails. It is a way of meeting the other person, whether things are going well or things are going poorly.

Unfortunately, there are no easy steps or a set of nifty tips that will ensure success, so what can we do? I believe it's best to base our actions on some fundamental principles, knowing that the exact words we use, the precise timing, and the back-and-forth dance with the other person will vary depending on far too many uncontrolled variables to ever predict. These principles give us a foundation that allows us to keep our wits, even when things get tough.

PRINCIPLES OF ENGAGEMENT

How do we stay excited about our idea and stay engaged with the other person? We may fear that paying attention to the other person will cause us to lose sight of our own goals. Somehow we will be swallowed in this touchy-feely morass and never accomplish anything. Those are sound fears. We need a way to engage — to be fully interested in the other person's views while sticking with what's important to us.

PRINCIPLES OF ENGAGEMENT

Know Your Intention
Consider the Context
Avoid Knee-Jerk Reactions
Pay Attention
Explore Deeply
Find Ways to Connect

I have identified six principles that can be helpful in developing understanding, favorable reactions, and building trust. When you apply the principles in your exchanges with others, I believe you will increase your ability to get things done. You should find that you are more successful in meeting your goals, while also building stronger relationships with those you wish to influence. And in those instances when you don't succeed, the principles can help you determine why things didn't work out. Using the principles, you may find that you can go back to these people with a different approach and obtain a much better outcome.

Here is a brief summary of the principles of engagement. In part II of this book I will explore each of these principles more deeply.

Know Your Intention
Since our intentions guide our actions, I believe it is important to have a clear intention in mind before engaging another person.

Every year I receive a call from Carla, a telemarketer who represents a non-profit I support. She begins by asking about me. And I believe she actually cares about how I respond. I believe this because what she says next is in direct response to what I said. She actually listens! She tells me about the work of the group and is sensitive to how much information I want to hear. One year, I had to cut back the donation. I didn't hear a scripted rebuttal telling me why her organization was more important than my mortgage payment. In fact, I didn't get a rebuttal at all. I got a thank you for my continued support. I continue to donate to the organization, and each year I welcome her call.

Some people are idea people. They are movers and shakers. They get things done. Others focus on relationships with others. They are keenly attentive to nuance. They are sensitive to the needs of the other person. Being just one way or the other can create problems. When we only pay attention to the idea we are trying to sell, we run the risk of alienating others and creating show-stopping resistance. When we rely on just the relationship with others, we may see our effectiveness diminish. People may like us, but they seldom accept our ideas.

Paying equal attention to both allows us to expand the possibilities. I am not advocating a watered down "let's both give in a little bit" approach. While this can be effective in little things, it is a dangerous first choice when you really care about your idea. If your dream is to live in California and your spouse prefers New York, choosing a point halfway between like Kansas (as nice as that state may be) is not a suitable solution.

Clear intention can be like a lighthouse beacon. Even when you begin to lose your way, you can look up and see it through the fog. Think of those times when your emotions are so strong that they cloud your vision. In those moments, it is easy to lose sight of the living, breathing person sitting across from you; all you may care about is yourself and perhaps your idea. The clearer your intention, the easier it will be to stick with the other person when the going is tough. Chapter 4 covers this principle.

Consider the Context
Context is critical. The idea itself is only part of the issue. It is possible to forget that time, place, and relationship are important parts of the equation as well. We might ask, "How will our history together affect his support? What else is going on in

his life? What's his experience with similar ideas?" We must step into others' shoes and consider our own idea from their vantage points. In addition, we need to look at how our own style helps and hinders our cause.

Felix Grant was one of the great jazz disk jockeys. For twenty-five years he had a nightly show on AM radio in the competitive Washington, D.C., market. As he thought about how station management and advertisers might receive a jazz program, he knew they would see this music as too big a financial risk. Surely the listeners they coveted would not listen to such lowbrow music. He had to consider how he approached the station management. In the late 1950s, long-playing records were gaining in popularity, so he called his show "The Album Sound." Grant says, "I dealt with them in the beginning by never using the word *jazz*. I would play Sinatra, who was very big then, but I would play the hipper things that nobody else was playing . . . and the non-jazz fan, for the most part, wouldn't really know it was jazz. He just heard good music, music that wasn't played much anywhere else. And it worked out very well. They sold a lot of spots and the station was happy."[1]

Chapter 5 gives you detailed guidance on applying this principle.

Avoid Knee-Jerk Reactions

It helps to avoid responding instantly and instinctively when people resist us. These automatic knee-jerk reactions often make matters worse. Although we cannot stop the involuntary defense that comes when someone attacks us or our idea, we can keep ourselves from doing damage by reacting without thinking first.

The six principles allow us to determine if people understand us, are reacting favorably or unfavorably to our idea, and gauge the level of trust between us.

Recently, I received an unsolicited call from a salesperson at a brokerage house. He began by asking me about my financial situation. I told him that I don't give out that information to people I don't know. He continued, "Are your investments making 25 percent a year?" I didn't respond. He kept on talking.

I told him I wasn't interested. His voice started to change. It sounded more strident. He spoke faster and louder. He told me I was a fool and said that he was so successful he really didn't need my business. He pushed and tried to prod. I told him I was going to hang up. "No, no, no. You can't do that." And he made yet another selling point. Finally, I did hang up. It was only my genetically programmed Midwestern politeness (and a little bit of curiosity) that kept me on the phone at all. He started poorly and only made matters worse for himself by talking too much and insulting me.

The danger of knee-jerk reactions is that they invite a knee-jerk reaction in response. I began to close down within the opening moment of the call. As he continued to speak, I built a wall. And once he insulted me, he could have made the greatest investment offer of the century, and I would not have responded.

Rachel had a similar experience with an investment advisor. He had all the answers and didn't seem terribly interested if they actually fit her questions. He overwhelmed her with his own force of reason, no matter that his logic had little to do with her needs. In stark contrast, another investment salesperson called just to check in. He didn't push or try to sell. As they talked, he suggested meeting for lunch. They did. He listened and listened. He made suggestions based on what Rachel had been saying. He now handles her portfolio.

In chapter 6, I will cover a broad range of knee-jerk reactions. We will explore ways to stop ourselves before we put a foot in our mouths — and what to do to extract feet during those times when our knees work faster than our brains.

Pay Attention
As we present our idea, we need to be alert. We need to pay attention to how others respond to us and to the idea itself. Listen to others' words and tone of voice. Notice the way they shift their bodies and whether or not they are making eye contact. During a broadcast of a Super Bowl, sportscaster Pat Summerall once said, "If only faces could talk." Well, they can, Pat. And we can learn a lot from them.

Also, we need to pay attention to our own reactions. Note shifts in our emotions, physical changes such as increased muscle tension, and thoughts that are evoked by others' response to our brilliant idea.

Jack Lemmon said, "The difference between Walter Matthau and other actors is that he acts with you and not at you. An awful lot of actors really don't act with you. . . . They're sitting there waiting for their line. . . . They're listening for a cue. But they're not listening to you. They're listening to the words. . . . Listening is not listening to the words, it's listening to the person."[2]

Matthau was a master of the principle of paying attention. Watch good actors at work. They respond to whatever occurs in front of them. A partner says a line with a different emphasis in tonight's performance or misses a cue and the good actor responds appropriately. Good actors do this because they know how to pay attention.

In contrast, there is a story about an actor in the decades-old London production of *The Mousetrap*. In the script, she enters and walks downstage and screams when she sees a body on the floor. One night, the body was placed in a different location. The actor entered, walked downstage, and looking directly at an empty floor, screamed.[3]

Much of the training an actor receives is based on refining his or her ability to observe. Many of the ideas covered in chapter 7 come from the acting profession.

Explore Deeply

When people oppose us or our ideas, it is important to be willing to find out why. Their initial reaction probably will not tell you the true reasons why they don't like an idea, but this is the information we need to hear in order to find out whether there is a way we can agree to move forward.

Unfortunately, the words people use may mask their true opinions and feelings. It is possible that they themselves don't even know why they resist. Gentle but persistent exploration into the heart of the resistance may be the only reliable way to transform opposition into support for your idea.

Author and consultant Peter Block suggests that we shouldn't bother listening in meetings, because people never say what's on their minds. With tongue in cheek, he encourages us to hang out in restrooms on breaks, because that's where the real conversations take place. We need to bring these restroom conversations out in the open.

As you begin to explore Level 2 and Level 3 issues, you may find that your own Level 2 and Level 3 fears block your ability to pay attention. The "fear response" gets in the way. Chapter 8 covers ways to stay open to deeper exploration of reactions to you and your idea.

Find Ways to Connect

This principle focuses on ways to meet our own goals while also addressing others' fears and helping them meet their goals. The challenge is keeping our goals and theirs in mind at the same time. This is not a time to back off and dilute our idea. However, it is a time to push ourselves to be as expansive in our thinking as possible. Working with the other person, we can explore a critical question: "How can both of our goals be met?" The answer to that question is probably not immediately apparent or else we would have thought of it already. We need to keep exploring. It is only in this creative process of exploration that we can find out whether a mutual win is possible.

When we seek mutual gain, look for any possible common ground. In April 1998, U.S. Attorney General Janet Reno, a strong proponent of gun control, spoke to a group of gun dealers. She began, "I don't care which side of the gun issue you're on; we all can agree that unsupervised use of guns by children must be stopped."

Her opening statement was unusual in two significant ways. It was an invitation that asked adversaries to join her in dialogue. And it framed the problem in a way acceptable to both sides. The statement was important for what it didn't say as well. It did not accuse, threaten, or give an ultimatum. It simply provided a common starting point for discussion between those who advocate complete freedom when it comes to gun ownership and those who push for abolition or registration of firearms.

Chapter 9 explores a variety of ways to connect your aspirations and ideas with others'. Later chapters will explore how to minimize harmful resistance before problems occur, making it much easier to apply the principles listed above.

THE PRINCIPLES IN ACTION

On January 22, 1999, United Flight 621 sat on the runway at Washington's Reagan National Airport for four hours waiting for clearance to take off for O'Hare. At 6:00 p.m. the plane rolled back to the terminal. The flight was cancelled due to poor weather conditions in Chicago. Usually this maddening delay would cause people to get testy and mean. Just two weeks before, passengers who waited for nine hours on a Northwest flight made headlines when their anger exploded onto the front pages of newspapers across the United States. As bathrooms overflowed, the passengers became unruly. People threatened the airline crew. Later, they brought suit against the airline. On United 621, I don't recall seeing anyone show anger toward the crew or other passengers. People shared cell phones. Joked. Talked. Worked.

The principles of engagement can assist us in gaining understanding, favorable reactions, and trust — and they can lessen the harmful impact of resistance at all three levels.

The pilot on the United flight was a model of the use of the principles of engagement. Minutes after the plane taxied onto the tarmac, he came out of the cockpit and said something like: "Folks, I'm the captain. Normally, you wouldn't see me this early in the flight. You might think something's wrong, and you'd be right. Chicago is socked in with fog. Planes all across the country are in the same situation as we are. We don't know how long this fog will last, but I hope it will clear soon. We could go back to the gate, but I'd rather not. We're second for takeoff, and if we go to the gate, we not only get behind every plane here, but all the planes on the East Coast. Please bear with me."

Every thirty minutes he made an announcement, even if he had no news. In between announcements, he walked up and down the aisles. He answered questions when he could, but mostly he listened.

Imagine that his goal was to get us to support him in his decision to sit on the runway. Of course, he could sit there all day without our permission, but if he had simply exerted his power as captain, he might have had an unruly group on his hands and his airline might have lost customers. Instead, he seemed to embody the principles simply and elegantly.

Know Your Intention. Although we can't know what went on inside the captain's head, he probably thought about how he was going to approach the passengers before he entered the main cabin. His experience certainly told him that how he engaged with passengers would be critical. I imagine that he knew that we were all in this together and that he would be well served to treat us with respect.

Consider the Context. People would want information. They would want to ask questions — and have them answered. They would want to be kept informed of weather conditions. He had to know that tempers could flare.

Avoid Knee-Jerk Reactions. I never heard him defend himself or the airline. After a few hours of responding to the same questions, it wouldn't be surprising to see someone lose his or her cool. He didn't.

Pay Attention. He listened and listened to passengers. His comments always seemed to be in response to what they asked or concerns that they raised.

Explore Deeply — and Find Ways to Connect. Often these two principles work in concert. Sometimes it is difficult to tell where one ends and the other begins. Walking the aisles three hours into an indefinite delay would make many pilots apoplectic. When you give people bad news, you can't predict how they will respond. It would have been so easy for him to remain safely inside the cockpit and to let the flight attendants deal with whatever the passengers did. He chose to mingle. From his first announcement, he kept telling us he wanted to help all of us get to Chicago as fast as possible. He linked his goal with ours.

When someone like this airline pilot wants us to support his plan to sit on a runway for hours, the process seems so natural and so effortless. But ask yourself, how many delayed flights have you been on that could have benefited from someone like him? For most of us, applying the principles doesn't come quite so naturally.

If we were pilots, after two hours of hearing the same yapping, we might become sarcastic or short in our replies: "Hello? Weren't you listening? Didn't I just say that?" The principles can help us before we say things that might make matters worse. If we recognize our own knee-jerk responses in all their subtle manifestations, we can stop ourselves before we go too far.

A PATH TO MASTERY

Staying excited and engaged is a lifelong challenge. Just when I think I've got it, something happens to assure me that I don't. When a flight cancels and the gate agent doesn't seem to care, when a customer service rep refuses to listen to a repair problem, or when I am put into a voicemail system designed by Dante — "Dial nine if you ever hope to leave this voicemail hell" — I may forget to use the principles.

> The philosopher Schopenhauer once said that it is in the trivial moments when we are off guard that we best show our character.

Throughout the book I use a variety of examples to illustrate mastery as well as less effective practice. Some of these examples are on the world stage where lives hang in the balance; others are tiny and may seem almost inconsequential. I believe we can learn as much from how a flight crew responds to a delayed flight as we can from how a world leader responds to challenges. I think we can learn as much from the trivial as from the profound.

It's probably best to think of work on the principles as the pursuit of mastery. Few people who we might think are at the top of their games will ever refer to themselves as masters. They know that perfection is always just a step ahead of them. I suspect that Walter Matthau remained attentive to the challenge of "acting with" throughout his career.

INTERVIEW WITH
SENATOR GEORGE MITCHELL

Former United States Senator George Mitchell was independent chairman of the peace talks in Northern Ireland that resulted in the 1998 Good Friday peace accords. When the talks began, the divide separating Protestants and Catholics seemed insurmountable, and each side had factions, each with its own interests. Since Mitchell had been chosen by the British and Irish governments, some already were suspicious of his ability to do this job fairly. In *Making Peace*, Senator Mitchell tells the story of that process. I was interested in his personal story. How did he stay calm in the face of so much pressure? How did he avoid lashing out or just leaving when he was under attack or failure seemed imminent?

RM: When you were about to take your place as a chair of the peace process, Ian Paisley, head of the Democratic Unionist Party, stood up and shouted, "No! No! No!" repeatedly and then stormed out with his contingent. During all this you remained outwardly calm. How did you do that?

GM: Obviously, I was apprehensive. It was an unusual circumstance, unlike anything I had ever before encountered. But I had long experience as senate majority leader in difficult and sometimes controversial situations. I learned that when you get upset or lose your temper or get emotional, you place yourself at a disadvantage. Thinking and speaking clearly is the most effective way to respond. Remain calm and think things through. I didn't surrender to the temptation to simply leave, but rather determined to see it through.

RM: I am amazed at how you reacted throughout the process. The challenges didn't seem to be limited to one or two instances. Tension seemed to be in the air for most of the twenty-two months of the process.

GM: There were many such occasions. By definition, these are difficult circumstances. I entered the process with the knowledge that it was a very difficult emotional situation, one in which there was little prospect of success and there would be many opportunities for failure or setback. One time that I came close to giving vent to my anger and disgust was in December of 1997. Just before Christmas we tried to reach an agreement on a statement of the principal questions facing the negotiators, and we couldn't even get agreement on that! The meeting degenerated into an acrimonious finger-pointing and name-calling session, and it seemed like things regressed back to what it had been for the previous eighteen months. I was very angry and thought about telling them in no uncertain terms what I felt. But, after thinking about it while they were continuing the discussion, I concluded that it wouldn't serve any purpose at that point. I couldn't reverse the events of that day, and I'd do best to try to prepare them for a more positive return when we came back from the Christmas break.

RM: In your book *Making Peace*, you discussed the importance of making a plan and sticking to it "while retaining the flexibility to make adjustments as circumstances change."
GM: That type of planning is quite common in the political process, particularly at the present time, when the pressure from the media puts political leaders in a situation of having to respond to every problem, challenge, or concern instantly. The notion that you should sit down and study and think about a problem doesn't seem to be acknowledged or accepted at all. I think you have to be careful and prudent and have enough self-confidence that you cannot panic at the first sign of adversity, but take the time to think through the consequences of what you're doing and what the adverse reaction is or might be to any further comments you might make.

RM: You also said, "I always find it useful to subject my actions to analysis of those who disagree with me."
GM: I attempted to evaluate the actions that I had taken through the prism of those who were outspoken in their opposition to my serving as chairman. How would they see it? What would be their reaction to it? Would they be justified in drawing a negative conclusion? I think it's a fine art because you have to have a balance. You can't be paralyzed by your enemies, in this case, those who are opposed to the peace process. I could not let their opposition immobilize me or the proceedings. At the same time, if any agreement was to be credible and have any chance of gaining public

INTERVIEW WITH SENATOR GEORGE MITCHELL (continued)

support, it had to be done in a fair and appropriate manner, with careful consideration given to the views of those who opposed the process. Just because people were opposed to the process didn't mean that every view they advanced was wrong. It's always helpful to try to put yourself in the mind of someone who disagrees with you to first judge whether or not your actions are in fact correct and, if not, to correct them. But also, if you feel that your actions are correct, being able to see the situation from the other perspective helps you to respond to criticism effectively.

RM: You mentioned that gaining trust and confidence was far more critical than any formal authority you were given.
GM: I was the beneficiary of the very length of the process. I didn't realize it at the time — and I certainly didn't feel grateful about it — but the negotiations lasted nearly two years. Through the way I handled myself and my performance, I was able to gain the confidence of the parties in a way that would not have occurred in a much shorter process. I began more as an impartial arbiter than as a mediator and negotiator. My role gradually transformed into the latter at the very end of the process, after I had gained their confidence. For most of the twenty-two months that the negotiations lasted, I acted more like a federal judge would act in presiding over a contentious proceeding; I had to make hundreds of decisions which I tried to do as fairly and as impartially as I could. Over time, I gained the sense that the participants felt that I was doing it in a fair and impartial and reasonable way and became more comfortable with me and more trusting.

PART II

Principles of Engagement

CHAPTER 4

Know Your Intention

It is the stretched soul that makes music, and souls are stretched by the pull of opposites — opposite bents, tastes, yearnings, loyalties. Where there is no polarity — where energies flow smoothly in one direction — there will be much doing but no music.

— Eric Hoffer, philosopher

Uri Savir, Israel's chief negotiator with the PLO, and his counterpart from the PLO, Ahmed Qurei, known as Abu Ala, made their cases. When Savir heard Ala compare Israel to Goliath and Palestine to David, he thought, "As in so many conflicts, each side considers itself the victim."

Savir said, "You are a threat because you want to live in my home. In my house."

"Where are you from?" Abu Ala asked. Savir replied that he was from Jerusalem. Ala asked where his father was from.

Savir said, "Germany."

Ala said his own father was born in Jerusalem.

"Why don't you ask about my grandfathers and their forebears?" Savir replied angrily. "We could go back to King David."

They were off to a tense start.

And then Savir said, "I'm sure we can debate the past for years and never agree. Let's see if we can agree about the future."

Abu Ala quietly said, "Fine."

This was their first understanding: They had agreed to focus on the future. This intention agreed to by both also served both sides in the subsequent talks.[1] Having such a strong commitment to focus on the future was especially helpful in an arena where, in Savir's terms, both sides saw themselves as victims.

Intention is the way we choose to engage the other person. Are we looking out for ourselves and seeing the other person as a potential obstacle? Or do we look out for our own wishes while taking a keen interest in the other person?

Our thoughts guide what we choose to do and this intention has the power to transform situations. If Savir and Abu Ala had chosen to focus on their own pasts, that intention would likely have limited their exchanges to a competition over whose ancestry gave them the rights to the land. If they had focused on just their own group's interests, they would probably have argued points without ever listening to the other side. However, by agreeing to focus on the future, they open the door for a very different type of conversation, one in which they can create something new.

An intention that focuses on our wants as well as those of the other person has a much greater chance of gaining support.

Too often we limit our intention to just our own interests. We want what we want, or we want to defend our turf, or we want to make someone else do something. This narrow intention makes it difficult for others to take an interest in what we want.

I AND YOU

Martin Buber developed a simple and elegant model that describes a way to create an intention that focuses on what we want while treating the other person with respect. He called it I/You — and I/It.[2] In Buber's scheme, to say the word "I" implies a relationship: I in relation to something or someone else. I own this computer. I drink from this cup. I am Kathy's husband. I work with John. I can be in relation to an It, such as a computer or cup, or I can be in relationship to a You, such as Kathy or John. The danger comes when we confuse a You for an It — when we turn the other person into an object, or an It.

Here's how it happens. Every time I want you to accept my idea and *enlist* your support, I risk turning you into an It. If all I care about is getting you to go along without question or fuss,

I am turning you into an It. In effect, I am saying that I don't care about you. You are simply a box to be checked off on my way to approval of a plan or a line item on my sales report.

I can only influence or be influenced by another You. I cannot influence my cup to run to the kitchen and get me some more coffee. I've tried; it doesn't work. Whenever I try to sell you on an idea and all I care about is your signature or money or vote, I risk turning you into an It. On the other hand, an I/You relationship implies that we can influence one another.

People, unlike coffee cups, have desires and fears and interests. Most often, when people influence you to do something big — and even when thinking back on it you still think you made the right decision — they've somehow spoken to something churning inside you. You bought the life insurance because you truly believed that your family needed that protection — not just because someone used a scare tactic on you. You got fully behind a corporate reorganization because you believed it was the best way for your company to regain competitive advantage and it offered the best hope for you to keep your job. In those instances, people addressed what was important to you. Either they listened to you carefully or had some other way of knowing what was important to you. And perhaps they changed their own thinking in some way, based on what you told them.

A clear I/You intention is the beacon that allows us to stay focused on seeking understanding, gaining a favorable reaction, and building trust. If we keep I/You in mind, we can tell when we are about to veer off course.

I AND IT

In I/You exchanges people can be touched and influenced by what you tell them. There is a mutual exchange in an I/You relationship. This, unfortunately, is not the norm.

I see lots of people in my work — executives, salespeople, team leaders, consultants, and seminar leaders — who seem far more interested in presenting their ideas than in making contact with the people they are trying to influence (You's). All they want is for some person or group to accept their idea — their It. They have a message that assumes they have a right answer to something and it is their job to convey that message to the unenlightened. In those moments, they turn their audiences into Its. They want to do something *to* someone else, but aren't interested in being influenced in return. The recipients of the I/It attack can be an audience of one or a room filled to overflowing.

What is common is that someone is treating another person or people as an object. For example:

- When your boss asks your opinion on something that has already been decided, you've become an It.
- When a salesperson would rather make his quota than make sure you get what you need, you have become an It.
- When a co-worker from another department invites you to a meeting, and it is clear that you are there as a token representative of your own group, you have become an It.
- When a husband holds onto an idealized picture of what a wife should be, in spite of her comments that she doesn't fit that picture, she has become an It. And vice versa.
- When a disagreement with someone over a point escalates into each side simply repeating his or her position over again, adding new selling points with each telling, these people have lost contact with one another and are only interested in getting the idea across — each of them has become an It.

When people are treated like Its, they probably don't say to themselves, "She's treating me like an It. I don't like that." But the impact is just the same. Most of us deeply resent being turned into an object. Consider how you react when people treat you like an It.

We need a way to see the other person and our own desires with equal clarity. Too often we are adept at just the I part, and so the other person becomes the It that stands between our objective and us.

Consider the examples listed above and how they all might have been different if the person had considered I and You — the idea and the other person — with equal value. What if your boss had asked your opinion and was willing to seriously consider what you said? In the end, your boss might agree or disagree with your thinking, but you'd know that you were taken seriously. Or imagine a salesperson who listened carefully to what you wanted and was even willing to suggest a less expensive item based on your needs? In these instances, your attitude about the exchange and the final decision would probably have been significantly different. It is likely that you would be more inclined to trust that person in the future, and to seek ways to understand what he or she is saying.

It would be nice if there were a few easy steps to follow that would guarantee that we could keep I and You in mind and ensure that we can stay excited about our idea and stay engaged with the other person. But predictable orderly steps only work when we are dealing with Its, say assembling a new bicycle. Linear and predictable don't fit I/You relationships. When we treat each other as a You instead of an It, we are often surprised. And surprise has its own logic. The joy and sometimes the agony of relationships is embedded in this surprise.

As we engage others with an intention of holding onto both I and You, we have the opportunity to learn about them and about ourselves. These exchanges can't be scripted. But before you roll your eyes, this I and You business isn't as foreign or counter-cultural as it might seem. Think about a relationship you enjoy with a close friend. Whenever you meet, the conversation flows in unexpected and exciting directions. You leave knowing a little more about your friend and perhaps a little more about yourself. The entire conversation seemed effortless. Most of us have experienced this willingness to take an interest in a friend without abandoning ourselves. Remembering these exchanges can serve us when we are trying to influence someone else. It is precisely this level of interest and willingness to be influenced ourselves that creates the conditions needed to influence others.

> "We have to hear a whole lot more before we jump to conclusions."
> — *Phil Chenier, sportscaster, referring to alleged misconduct by a player*

THE POWER OF SHIFTING FROM I/IT TO I/YOU

Ala and Savir could have spent hours, even days, discussing history, wrongs that had occurred in the past, and made demands of each other. All of these statements would have been from strong I positions with little consideration of the other side. Jointly deciding to focus on the future shifted their attention from strictly I to I and You.

Extending our goal to include the other person may take some thought and practice. Intention, as I use the term in this book, is a shift from I/It to I/You. Making that shift is no small thing, but I believe that shift alone can transform how we approach other people. If I meet you with an intention of engaging you as a You, the questions I ask, the statements I make, the pauses I allow for you to react, will be significantly different than if I approach you as an It.

Gail is an expert in business communications and has developed materials and key phrases that help create her market identity. One of her clients (let's call him Chet) included some of Gail's ideas in an article he wrote, without giving her credit. Gail felt it was important to protect her brand and wanted to ensure that this wouldn't happen again.

She sent him a friendly note. Nothing happened. So she called him. He bristled. He claimed that she was overreacting. The conversation ended in an impasse, and Gail was at risk of losing a client.

She realized that she was going to have to bring this up once again, and she was not looking forward to it. She was at risk of falling into some knee-jerk reaction and just going after him. But then she thought about her intent. She wanted to make sure her materials weren't used without proper attribution; she also wanted to keep the relationship strong. She told me, "We had a long-standing business relationship that was good for both of us."

She shifted her intent to I/You. She thought about what was most important to her: "I want to continue our strong working relationship in a way that serves both of us. As long as he didn't continue to use my materials without giving me credit, I could let that matter drop." She arranged to meet with Chet to discuss the issue again.

"The meeting was hard," Gail said, "but I kept my intent in mind throughout. Even though I brought up my concern about my ideas being used, I did it in a way that he could hear. I even had notes in front of me that included key phrases such as 'I could understand how this could happen . . . it certainly would be easy to overlook . . . I bet you didn't realize . . .' — phrases that would show I was totally on his side."

"He apologized and asked whether I'd like for him to publish a retraction. I said that wasn't necessary, that I only wanted to protect my ideas. I told him I was most concerned about keeping our working relationship strong."

When we feel we have been injured, it is easy to forget the You. This plays out in how people use our legal system much of the time. Nancy Lasater is a trial attorney. She couldn't understand why people couldn't just sit down and talk over their problems. "Sometimes the rules and gladiator fighting became paramount. I've had clients come in for litigation, and I say, 'You don't want to litigate this, you want to solve it.' And they say, 'What's the difference?'"[3] So she helps her clients create an intent that better serves their real purpose: "My key orientation is that what really matters to the clients is getting the problem solved at the least possible cost and trying to preserve the business relationship."

GUIDELINES FOR GETTING STARTED

Here are a few guidelines that can help you examine what you intend and create an intention statement that shifts the focus to I/You.

Focus on Issues Instead of Positions
Sometimes our intention may be too narrowly defined. Persuading a teenager to study, making the sale, even reorganizing the office are focused on a single outcome that we want. In *Getting to Yes*, Roger Fisher and William Ury distinguish between positions and interests. A *position* is clear but limits our options. "I want to reorganize" or "I want to sell you the super deluxe model" is limited to a binary response: Either I get my way or I do not. If the other person doesn't like my position, we are probably in for a fight. While strong positions

POLITICS ARE REAL

Any book that suggests you pay attention to people along with your idea may seem soft and mushy. It could seem that attention to I/You ignores the fact that we live in a world where office politics (and family politics) are real. If we were to ignore the competition, secrecy, and conflict that are at least a part of most organizations, we would enter conversations naïvely. We would be setting ourselves up for ridicule and failure. At best, we would be less effective getting things done. At worst, we would be ignored as someone others could afford to ignore.

Because most organizations are political, it is almost impossible to engage in serious discussions without paying attention to the strategies you will use to engage others. But strategy — the overall planning and conduct of how you will proceed — can be used in two very different ways. When we think of strategy, we may picture an I/It world in which Machiavelli (*The Prince*), Sun Tzu (*The Art of War*), and Clausewitz (*On War*) reign. All of these writers focus on winning. While they acknowledge that it is better to avoid war when possible, armed conflict is always a close possibility. They offer little to suggest an I/You alternative. It's almost as if they are saying, "Try to do it nicely, but be prepared to do battle."

Some of the principles — such as pay attention, avoid knee-jerk reactions, explore deeply, and find ways to connect — encourage you to focus on how you are meeting the other person. That's strategy, but it looks very different than if your intent were merely to sell your idea. For example, some books on sales and influence show you how to determine the other person's personality type, not to communicate more deeply with them, but to get the upper hand. I suggest using strategy for a different purpose, one that furthers movement in a direction toward I/You.

Without a strong commitment to I/You, our approach to strategy will be limited to options that result in conflict sooner rather than later. During a protracted struggle, without a belief in an I/You approach, it is simply too difficult to have the courage to stick with another person for very long. For example, in the United States, we have become increasingly litigious. It is one thing for a marriage to break up; it is another for it to end up in a protracted court battle. It is almost as if we can't even envision strategies that don't involve someone winning and someone losing.

Attention to I/You is so radical that we may only accept it as an outer garment to be discarded quickly when things begin to get hot. We promise ourselves we'll use it where it is easy and forget about it all the other times. I believe I/You can even guide our actions in highly political environments.

But what if others try to take advantage of our openness? They see a willingness to be influenced as a sign of weakness, and they use that to force you to give up things that are important to you. In that situation, we risk losing our I. We allow ourselves to be so focused on the other person — on the You — that we forget the equation has both I and You. Keeping the intention in mind can help keep the proper balance.

So perhaps in that instance, I realize that I can't afford to be as open as I would like. That doesn't suggest that I then need to revert to I/It. I can still treat you with dignity and respect and wait to see whether there is a better time or place to engage more openly. Acting with awareness allows me to see when I can afford to be a little less strategic in my exchanges with others.

I/You is an ideal and not one that is easily met. However, just moving toward that ideal can make a difference in the quality of our relationships and the types of support we can build. If we were to work toward the ideal (knowing that we live in a world in which strategy will be important in some situations), I believe we'd begin to find more places where richer person-to-person contact was possible. This could result in stronger working relationships, and our ability to influence and be influenced would increase.

Moving toward the ideal of I/You would put those instances of unhealthy political activity in sharp relief. We can begin to see those times when sticking with I/You might actually change the field we play on. We can see those times when explicitly wearing I/You is risky.

can help you determine what you want, Fisher and Ury say, "positional bargaining fails to meet the basic criteria of producing a wise agreement, efficiently and amicably."[4]

Traditional union and management bargaining pitted position against position in gladiator struggles to the death. Many negotiators now use an approach that allows all sides to state issues that are most important without first getting locked into positions. Fisher and Ury suggest that focusing on *interests* gives us more opportunities to create mutually beneficial results. For example, instead of expressing the goal as "I want to reorganize the office," reframe it as "I am concerned that our current way of working is inefficient and doesn't allow quick response to customers." This may be an issue that most can agree with. You give others more room to join you in conversation.

Staying open to the interests of your side and theirs is an important part of the I/You intention. In Nancy Lasater's case, her intention included the issues that she believes are important to her clients — solve the problem with as little cost as possible *and* try to save the working relationship.

Focus Long Term

If tensions are high — especially when Level 3 mistrust is high — it may be difficult to keep the intention in mind as you work. There may be times — even long periods of time — when the fog is so thick, you can hardly see your lighthouse. In these instances, it is critically important to think long term.

Jared and Connie are colleagues. Once they seemed to have a good friendship and were able to count on each other on work projects. Pressures at work have strained their relationship. They can hardly stand to speak to each other. Level 3 mistrust makes each meeting difficult. And yet, both want something better, since they had it before. When they meet, they both keep an intention of I/You in mind. This makes a difference. Connie said, "That simple focus keeps me from blurting out the list of transgressions I think he should apologize for. It keeps me from responding sarcastically to some of his comments, and when I remember the You part of the I/You, I listen better."

Uri Savir and Abu Ala did not expect that the future would change for the better overnight, but their intention gave them a way to go forward. Gail's intention regarding Chet's use of her material was long term. Even if her meeting with him had failed, she might have come back another time with the same intention. However, if she stuck with her position that she'd been wronged and wanted Chet to make things right, she might have severed her relationship and possibilities for further work. She might even have won a lawsuit, but to what

ACT "AS IF"

But what about those times when it is difficult to even imagine focusing on the other person? A highly influential teacher of actors, Konstantin Stanislavski, suggested using the magic "as if."

Imagine that the actors playing Romeo and Juliet are not attracted to each other in the slightest. Unless they can figure out how to show they are wildly infatuated with one another, no one in the audience will believe these kids are willing to risk everything for love. Stanislavski would suggest that the actor act "as if" he were attracted to Juliet. This amazingly simple bit of advice has saved many actors who needed to show love, hate, abandonment, and betrayal to another actor on stage. The same can work when we are engaged with someone at work. We can act "as if" we like the person. We could ask ourselves, "How might I act if I really respected or admired or liked that other person who usually drives me nuts?"

This "as if" tactic can help shift the focus from I versus You into a relationship that has the possibility of a strong I/You connection. We could act as if we truly cared about the person. And acting "as if" can sometimes keep us from reacting so quickly or forcefully when someone provides a potential trigger for our knee-jerk reactions.

end? By shifting her focus to the longer-term relationship, she was able to identify an intent that was more beneficial. Her shift to wanting a solid long-term working relationship gave them both room to move.

Without the right intention, things can get nasty and we can work against even our own best interests. Ron Shapiro is an agent who represents superstars like Cal Ripken, Jr. In *The Power of Nice*, he tells a sobering story. As Oprah Winfrey started to gain popularity, she dropped him and went with another agent. One of Shapiro's attorneys told him that she still owed them commissions. "On a strictly legal basis, he was probably right. My instinct told me to drop it, but I didn't follow my gut." His office sued and won. "We won a short-term gain, but lost long-term good will. Maybe we'd never have done business with Oprah again. After we sued, it wasn't even a question. That's humbling."[5] With a different intent — "I want to maintain a good relationship with Oprah Winfrey no matter who represents her" — he might have made different choices.

As you will see in the chapter on knee-jerk reactions, there are many things that can divert us from what we know in our gut to be the right course of action.

Focus on the Relationship

Focusing on larger issues and focusing long term assume an I/You focus. One way to test your commitment to this is to state what you hope to gain. If the statement is limited to "I want something" and ends right there, you may have overlooked the most important element in influencing others — their interests.

Savir and Abu Ala both wanted a better future. Even though it was not Gail's first thought when she saw that Chet had published her ideas under his own name, she quickly realized that both she and Chet would benefit from a good long-term working relationship. Her shift in thinking allowed the conversation to focus on ways to achieve a mutually agreeable future.

A clear intention that includes both I and You can have the power to transform the quality of our exchanges with others from negotiations on the world stage to even the most mundane circumstances.

Focus on What Can Be Observed

Intention is where you want to focus your attention while you work together. It lets you know if you are on track. Middle East negotiators could tell if they were keeping focused on the future. Each side had its own specific objectives for the negotiations; the intention simply gave them a way to behave while they discussed these wishes.

When both parties agree to the same intention or way of working with each other — for instance, focusing on the future — both are looking in the same direction. That can be a tremendous help. But often you may need to create your intention alone, as in Gail's case. Both ways can work.

Sometimes our intent (especially in small day-to-day situations) may be unconscious and, therefore, unknown to us. When things work well, we may not think about our intention in each of life's little exchanges with other people. But in situations where there might be some opposition, knowing our intent and adapting it to fit the circumstance could increase our chances of meeting our goals considerably.

If our intention is narrowly defined — say getting retribution — that's where we focus. If it is more expansive — showing concern for their interests as well — then that's now where we focus. A clear intention guides our thinking, allowing all manner of smaller goals and ways of working together to come into play. According to brain researchers, once we establish a goal, "An emotion triggers the cascades of sub-goals and sub-sub-goals that we call thinking and acting."[6]

CLARIFYING INTENTION ON THE FLY

It may seem as if clarifying intention is a time-consuming affair involving chanting and incense. Not so. In my Theater of Resistance class I set up a scene where one person must get on a plane but hasn't brought any of the required paperwork. The plane will leave soon, so there is little time to spare. Often these scenes deteriorate into confrontations. The would-be passenger tries to play high status: "I'll have you know that I am a Lifetime Platinum and Omnipotent Frequent Flyer with your airline . . ." and on it goes. Since agents cannot allow people to board without the proper paper or e-ticket, the scene usually ends with the omnipotent flyer standing alone, waving bye-bye as the plane takes off. It doesn't have to be that way. When the hypothetical travelers in these scenes take just a few seconds to put themselves in the agent's shoes, their response to the airline employee changes dramatically — and so does the outcome.

I received this note from my friend Lynne:

> When I went to the airport last week the exact scenario that you use in your improv class came up for me — but I was ready! My client had sent me my itinerary rather than the e-ticket so the check-in agent said, "No deal," even though I was in the computer.
>
> With great irritation he asked, "Want to buy another ticket now?"
>
> "Gosh, I don't," I said with a smile. "This has never happened to me before, but I bet you've seen it happen a lot. What would you recommend I do?" (asked earnestly and innocently).

He came up with the option to use his phone and call my client's travel agent and get them to change something in the computer so he could issue the ticket. Took about sixty seconds. I told him he, was a prince of a guy and a great help to travelers.

To make an I/You intention work, we need information about the agent. And when we are standing in line waiting our turn, we need it fast. There is no time to engage in a lengthy conversation. In fact, given the pressure that agents are under to close the doors on time, a conversation would probably increase their resistance to our request.

We could take just a moment and ask ourselves, "What does the world look like through the eyes of ticket agents?" We would probably see a picture that looks a lot different from the way the world looks through our own eyes. It's not hard to imagine a very tired and busy person who probably has been threatened repeatedly already today. He or she is probably thinking about just getting the people in this long line checked in as quickly as possible. Anyone who asks for something out of the ordinary just makes the agent's life more difficult and slows things down. That would lead to a lot of angry customers demanding that they get attention. We'd probably see that there is nothing in it for the agent to allow you to board the plane. Pointing fingers or whining simply won't do anything to change the agent's mind. But imagining what the world looks like through an agent's eyes gives us options. We can still choose to threaten or beg, or we might shift our thinking to consider the agent's needs as well.

"Actors" in my workshops find that a few simple changes can make a significant difference. They acknowledge that the agent is busy. They show that they realize the agent could get in trouble for breaking a rule — and suggest exploring alternatives that stay within the rules.

Focusing just on ourselves doesn't give the agent any reason to want to help us. When the frantic flyer shifts positions from I/It to I/You, the agent often says something like, "I'm not sure if I can help. Let me check in these other passengers and I'll call my supervisor over." No guarantee, but far better than the alternative. I've learned from the "actors" in my

MANTRA

Mantras can support the I/You focus. Keith Johnstone, author of *Impro*, uses mantras (silent repeated phrases) in his improvisation work with actors. I was part of a scene with Bec. We were to play roommates. The first time through we just created a simple domestic scene with one of us coming home from work. The second time we used the same lines, but Keith asked each of us to repeat a mantra to ourselves of "I hate you." Even though the words were the same, our bodies said otherwise. Our voices had edges on them. On the third try, we used the mantra "I love you." Same words, but, once again, we were different. The way we faced each other, our voices, our eye contact — virtually everything except the words was different. With the shifts brought on by the mantras, our attitudes toward one another shifted.

Imagine that this scene between Bec and me had been real life. The consequences of an "I hate you" mantra could be long-lasting, as could the implications of an "I love you" mantra.

It is not uncommon to go through life with implicit mantras running through our heads. These mantras color how we see other people and limit our ability to focus on I and You. Without even thinking about it, these unconscious mantras become our intent.

Rather than letting the fates determine our mantras, we could consciously create ways to approach our partners, just as Bec and I did in that scene. And yes ... it is easier to do it on stage than in tense scenes from real life.

classes and have been able to change non-refundable non-transferable tickets by simply shifting my intent to I/You.

Why would an airline employee do this? I believe they, like most of us, want to be helpful — and they, like we, respond to being treated like a human for a change.

MOVING FORWARD

Many of us run the risk of focusing exclusively on our own wants: "I want what I want when I want it." And if things begin to sour, we may believe that we'll automatically pick up signals when it's time to shift our intention to I and You and get out of trouble.

The worldly philosopher Yogi Berra once said that you could observe a lot just by watching. True, but what we pay attention to limits what we see. We may believe that our powers of observation are quite good. We don't miss a thing. If it's out there, we see it and hear it. Not so. In one experiment, people watched a videotape of people passing a basketball back and forth and were told to count how many times the ball was passed. After the one-minute tape, people were asked for their answers and then were asked if they saw anything unusual. Usually the answer was no. The psychologist played the tape again, and people were surprised to see a woman with a parasol strolling through the scene.[7]

If our focus is on getting people to go along with our idea, that may be all that we see. We may miss the parasol, and that could be a critical oversight. The remaining principles focus on the times when we are actually engaged with the other person. Clear intention will be an important guiding light as we attempt to consider the context, avoid knee-jerk reactions, pay attention, explore deeply, and find ways to connect with others.

CHAPTER 5

Consider the Context

I felt within me the need to become what I had been accused of being. . . .
I became the coward, traitor, thief [that] they saw in me.
— Jean Genet, *The Thief's Journal*

The recent history of South Africa is filled with its larger-than-life saints and villains. But deep within the country, far beyond the spotlight of international attention, is a heart that allowed the destruction of apartheid to happen relatively peacefully. In *Anatomy of a Miracle*, Patti Waldmeir writes about talking with an ANC member:

> "So, I ask, getting straight to the point, why don't you hate whites?"
>
> The young man replied, "There is no way I can hate whites. To hate whites would be unfair. . . . Our problem is not whites per se. Our problem is the system which made whites the culprits of apartheid."
>
> According to Waldmeir, his response was not a lone instance. She heard this young man's voice in every township across South Africa. For thirty years the ANC taught by "word and example that racism is off limits" and its message was deeply embedded.[1]

This young man understood something that many miss. Everything we do occurs in context.

Nelson Mandela also understood that context is critical. Certainly, after twenty-seven years in prison, he had every right to be bitter and filled with hate, but he said, "I always knew that deep down in every human heart, there was mercy and generosity. No one is born hating another person because of the color of his skin . . . people must learn to hate, and if they can learn to hate, they can be taught to love."[2] This understanding did not make him soft or any less resolute in his determination to fight against apartheid. But it did give him a broader perspective. While he was a prisoner at Robben Island, he did the unthinkable. He learned the Afrikaans language. Many of his companions were shocked. After all, this was the language of the oppressor. But Mandela did even more. He read Afrikaner history, philosophy, and poetry, and he insisted that others do the same.[3] He knew that in order to influence he had to understand these people deeply.

Had Mandela and others limited their thinking to just their own goal — ending apartheid — without understanding the culture, history, hopes, and fears of these people, they would have been less successful. Or they would have been limited to a winner-take-all contest with the enemy.

THE SIGNIFICANCE OF CONTEXT

Context is the ground we walk on. The better we understand the terrain, the more prepared we can be for the journey.

The more we understand the context in which we are trying to influence others to support our ideas, the better we will be able to determine the likelihood they will understand what we are saying, react favorably, or even trust us sufficiently to listen in the first place.

Everyone knows that walking on a beach is different from scrambling over rocks in an ascent up a mountain. We wear different shoes. We carry different clothing. We take different precautions. We seem to recognize the differences in the natural environment, but then assume that organizations and situations with other people are pretty similar. If we do differentiate, we look at personality differences and miss the larger contextual issues.

In *The Social Animal*, Eliot Aronson summarizes research about how people make meaning in social situations: "[M]ost people tend to overlook the importance of the situation in explaining behavior, preferring instead to explain other people's actions in terms of assumptions about their personalities and attitudes. In other words, most of us assume that people's attitudes do indeed forecast their behavior, and then we over-apply this belief in interpreting the behavior of others. We see attitude-behavior relationships even when they might not exist in reality."[4]

Context is critical in most situations when we want to influence someone else. In managing projects, negotiating team priorities, trying to influence our boss to take a different course, attempting to sell a product or service, getting in to see a key decision maker, or influencing decisions at home, ideas die because we fail to attend to context.

Without attention to context, I am left thinking only of I — about my own ideas and plans. If I pay attention to context, I begin to see the rich relationship between us — between the I and You. I begin to see that influence is far more than just *selling* an idea. In order to influence, I must *understand*. Like Mandela, I must understand your culture, your history, and your poetry.

WHAT WE CAN LEARN FROM SALES

As I reviewed articles and books on change, sales, negotiation, and influence, I found that a surprising number gave little, if any, attention to context. They offered advice on ways to achieve objectives, but failed to explore the impact context could have on the situation. I think this is dangerous. A reader can walk away believing that all he or she need do is follow some simple, one-size-fits-all steps and things will work out fine. Since the 1920s, many salespeople have been taught to handle objections and close the sale. Once you know the objections, you can counter with answers. And you are always trying to clinch the deal by asking for the order. This advice is presented as holy writ by many who teach and write about sales. As good salespeople and negotiators know so well, that advice is wrong.

Research in sales indicates that the advice on handling objections and closing sales is fine for selling small items like toasters, but fails miserably when it comes to larger items such as new software systems, home furnishings, or a car. Trying to close big sales often drives the potential customer away. Neil Rackham's studies show that successful salespeople know the context, and they know their customers well. Good sales take time — not to keep trying to close the sale, but to build trust. The customer needs to have confidence in you, must believe that you truly understand the implications of the challenges she faces, and must think that what you offer is the right fit.[5]

Bad advice on handling objections and closing sales isn't limited to the world of sales. Whenever I try to counter your objection with a nifty rebuttal or whenever I keep pushing for your commitment, I run the same risk salespeople do. I risk driving you away because I have failed to pay attention to the complex relationships among understanding, reactions, and trust.

THE ELEMENTS OF CONTEXT

Imagine that you are a middle manager in a new job. You've been given responsibility to come up with a plan that will assign office space as it becomes available. When an office with a window that looks out onto blue sky becomes open, this plan will offer guidelines on how to assign the space fairly. You think, "No problem," and you get to work on it. In fact, it will feel good to put an easy win under your belt so early in this new assignment. Because seniority worked in your last job as a way to make similar decisions, you base your plan on this proven approach.

Three weeks later you've come up with a stunning plan. It's simple, elegant, and fair. You present it to the team. But instead of applause and adulation that should be yours, you notice icy stares and muttering. Your plan dies the moment it is presented.

If you had looked through Level 2 (reaction) and Level 3 (trust) filters at the context, and asked a few questions, you might have come up with a different, and more successful, strategy.

Without asking, it would be hard to realize that there are land mines planted all over the office. There is a history of how office space was assigned in the past. Some still harbor grudges from these past oversights. An earlier plan was based on seniority, but it was so rife with political cronyism that the idea of seniority leaves a bitter taste in the mouths of many. And that's just the Level 2 reactions! Level 3 presents its own challenges. You represent all those lean and hungry managers who come in and try to make their mark by disrupting everything. If you had this knowledge when you accepted the assignment, you would probably have approached your task differently.

Level 2 Reactions to the Idea

Here are some larger contextual issues that show up in Level 2: history of the idea, your idea in conflict with their idea, the idea is a threat, word on the street, resilience versus burnout, and other bad timing issues.

We may be tempted to treat resistance to our ideas as Level 1 issues and simply give people more information. That works well if that's all people need, but it can fail if the issues are deeper.

History of the Idea

History puts its stamp on what we believe. Many ideas have a history, and people learn to believe certain things about those types of ideas based on their experience. Quality improvement is one of those ideas. In some organizations, quality efforts are appreciated because people have seen the value they have given in the past. In other organizations, quality has become a four-letter word. People invested time and commitment in it, only to see it fail. Now whenever anyone tries to initiate any type of quality improvement process, people roll their eyes. They feel they've been there already and are reluctant to go down that path again — no matter what promises anyone makes this time. I have seen people be reluctant to support an idea, even when they knew some change was needed, just because of the way this particular issue was handled in the past.

Ignoring the history of an idea can be a big mistake. No matter how glossy we make the presentation, if we don't acknowledge how this idea fared in the past, we risk failure. We need to address the unspoken objections that accompany the memory of that idea. Otherwise, we risk looking like we are naïve.

The leaders who say that a reorganization won't result in downsizing can't expect ready acceptance, unless they are able to demonstrate convincingly why this time will be different from all those botched attempts in the past.

Your Idea Is in Conflict with Their Idea

Sometimes our idea runs up against someone else's idea. When we get excited about our own thoughts, it is easy to forget that others have been thinking too. They have their own hopes, fears, and plans. This type of conflict can occur anywhere — for example, when parents decide that their oldest child should go to college at the old alma mater or the IT executive tries to get everyone in the corporation to switch to a different computer operating system. The conflict may have nothing to do with the quality of the college or the new computer system, but a lot to do with the fact that it goes against someone else's plans.

The Idea Is a Threat

As I mentioned in chapter 2, your idea may be a threat. People may be afraid that the idea will cost them something: They'll lose face, their job, recognition, or something else that they hold dear. Just because an idea looks good from where we sit doesn't tell us what it looks like through the eyes of others.

The Word on the Street

The CEO of a hospital in the Washington, D.C., area once told me that the biggest obstacle to change in his organization was the morning paper. His facility was well-managed and enjoyed fairly good cooperation between the administrators and medical personnel. However, people would learn about massive layoffs at other area hospitals from the morning paper and on local television news and start to worry. When the CEO spoke about the future of their hospital, staff would read in ominous warnings based on what they had heard about elsewhere.

Pay attention to what people know — and what they think they know — about your idea. People pick up information from the media, from friends who have just experienced something similar, and from the rumor mill. Even if the information is incorrect or doesn't apply to your unique situation, what people believe will drive what they do. If your idea seems dangerous to them, it is dangerous until you are able to demonstrate that it's not.

Resilience versus Burnout

In *Managing at the Speed of Change*, Daryl Conner suggested that lack of resilience is one of the major reasons why changes fail.[6] He was speaking of big organizational changes, but his wisdom applies to every situation in which we want to influence someone else. Sometimes people are just worn out. They may even love your idea, think it is the best thing that could happen, but they won't support it because they are just too tired. If you were to wait a month or two, conditions might be significantly different. Or if you were to suggest implementing the idea in small increments, you might have a more receptive audience.

Other Bad Timing Issues

Bob Beemer, perhaps the first person who noticed the potential Y2K problem, was a victim of bad timing. He made his discovery in 1969. The problem (if it was going to be a problem) was thirty-one years away. Computer memory was expensive and bulky. Companies needed to dedicate an entire room to this purpose. By 1998 conditions were different, and many were receptive to his message. Not only was computer memory cheap and easy to install, but the threat of clocks rolling over to 2000 was looming.

Sometimes ideas are presented in the wrong part of a business cycle. Companies seldom increase spending on training when they are in the midst of a financial struggle. Often they even decrease those funds. Imagine that you have a great idea for a major new educational program that could truly help your company be more competitive. People may love it and see the potential value, but because revenues are down, no one wants to take a risk and fund the project.

Individuals have internal timing issues as well. Sometimes people just need time to think about an idea. But because we want to move ahead, our pit bull tenacity takes over and we demand that they give us a response right now. Forcing the timing of a response can make someone say no when a week later he or she might have said yes. I have turned down salespeople just because they put pressure on me to buy immediately. They often use the scarcity ploy to put the pressure on: "This is the last one" or "The sale ends tonight." Even though I don't buy from them, I sometimes do buy the product later from one of their competitors.

Level 3 Trust Issues

These deep issues may come from your history together, what you represent, relative rank and status, effect of the environment on your relationship, and the impact of beliefs on relationships. All can have an impact on how receptive someone is to listening to an idea that you present.

Your History Together

Think about the person you want to influence. What would she say about you? Does she trust you? Does she think you are bright? Realistic? Does she think you have her best interests at heart? Does she think you have the best interests of her organization at heart? The answers to these questions could indicate whether or not you have sufficient rapport in your relationship to talk about your idea or let you know that there are serious Level 3 issues at play.

While Terry Anderson was held hostage in Lebanon, his relationship with a fellow hostage named David deteriorated. He asked two of the other hostages what was going wrong and what they suggested he do to make things easier. Anderson recalled that they "blasted" him, saying, "'You challenge David all the time. You seem to want to top him, to prove something to him. . . . ' I was shocked. Naturally, I'd assumed the others would agree with me that David was causing the trouble."

Anderson apologized, "If I've done things to offend you, I'm sorry. I'd like to start over." He assumed David would reciprocate and they'd shake hands. Instead, he replied, "Yes, you have. You've been a bastard."

Anderson said it was hard for him to accept the fact that he was seen as "argumentative, bullheaded, trampling over other people." To his credit, he reflected on the feedback and realized that, even if David were at fault too, he had to change if conditions were going to improve.[7]

What You Represent

Another variation on Level 3 has little to do with you personally and a lot to do with what you represent. Union and management, black and white, male and female, Protestant and Catholic in Northern Ireland, straight and gay, pro-life and pro-choice, and young and old are some of the differences that may appear as Level 3 trust issues and can impair clear vision. When others look at you through a Level 3 lens, they've already seen something they don't like in the group you stand for, so they are not likely to trust what you have to say.

Level 3 resistance occurs in relationship. If someone is looking at you through a Level 3 lens, you run the risk of failing to connect. He or she may be closely guarded and dismiss everything you say, while thinking, "What could you expect from someone like that?"

Relative Rank and Status

Status is the relative power differential between you and the other person. Status can come from differences in official rank, such as between a general and a private or a manager and a secretary. But actual rank is only part of it. Status can also come from differences in personal power. In theater, actors talk about playing high status or low.

Our relationships with others involve status. And status counts. We create elaborate dances that define these relationships. You might look at a couple of people around you and ask yourself, "Who is playing high status and who is playing low?" How can you tell? For starters, look at how they stand or sit relative to each other. Note if there a difference in how they speak — perhaps halting and breathless, or slow and assured.

As you read this, somewhere someone in a large organization is making a presentation of a rather good idea to someone or some group that is looking at the presenter through a Level 3 filter. Unless this person knows that Level 3 resistance is standing between them and begins to demonstrate that he is different from their perception, this new idea will probably fail.

If you are playing low status to the other person's high status, he or she will expect certain things from you. A certain deference perhaps. If you ignore this and cross that boundary, you will create a static interference that could get in the way of the person attending to you and your idea.

When lawyers argue before appellate judges, they are expected to stop talking the moment a judge says anything. Lawyers do not finish their sentences or override a judge's interruption. They wisely shut up. One lawyer forgot this and began his opening statement by saying, "I have three points to make, so please hold your questions until I finish." The judges played their status card and stopped him immediately. They told him that they would interrupt whenever they pleased. He heard the message. The status dance is not like 1960s rock; it is a carefully choreographed minuet, with each partner instinctively knowing his or her steps.

Following these written or unwritten rules is not the same as giving in. You can follow the rules and hold your own. A good lawyer will play by the status rules and disagree with a judge by stating arguments clearly, based in case precedent, at the appropriate time.

Self-esteem can differentiate status as well. Imagine you are a pretty confident person and you are working with someone who has lower self-esteem. Research indicates that people with low self-esteem can become so overwhelmed by fear that they cannot act until the pressure or fear becomes very strong.[8] If you are trying to influence someone who seems to have low self-esteem and you are a pretty confident and assertive person, you may run the risk of overwhelming the person and consequently getting resistance instead of support. Just noticing this difference may help you adjust how you approach this person, lessening the perceived status difference between you.

Context can have a strong impact on what people hear and how they hear it — and that includes us. Whether people understand, or react favorably, often rests on Level 2 and Level 3 issues.

You may find playing a status role unseemly. That may be, but you're doing it all the time anyway. Most work relationships are defined by differences in status. Some people have more power. Others less. Some take charge and others defer. Like it or not, it seems to be part of the human condition.

Keith Johnstone, who bases much of his theater improvisation work on status differences, tells this story: "A friend who played B movies became fascinated with status transactions: he played high to agents and directors (and they hated him); he played low and they loved him (but they didn't give him work); he matched status with them and they gave him leads in A movies."[9]

Status differences can interfere with clear communication. If both sides play their prescribed roles, it may be difficult for the low status person to influence the high status person (and sometimes vice versa, as in the low self-esteem situation described earlier).

The Effect of the Environment on Your Relationship

The effect of environment on our attitudes and behavior is not always positive. Philip Zimbardo created a mock prison in the basement of a building at Stanford University. By a toss of a coin, students were assigned roles as prison guards or prisoners.

After six days he had to close down the experiment "because what we saw was frightening. It was no longer apparent to us or most of the subjects where they ended and their roles began. The majority had indeed become 'prisoners' or 'guards,' no longer able to clearly differentiate between role-playing and self. There were dramatic changes in virtually every aspect of their behavior, thinking and feeling." Zimbardo and his colleagues say student guards treated the others "as if they were despicable animals, taking pleasure in cruelty" while the prisoners became "servile, dehumanized robots."[10]

The structure of an organization and the culture we live in influence behavior in dramatic ways. David Hanna's book on organizational change observes, "All organizations are perfectly designed to get the results they get."[11] In other words, if a company has dreadful customer service, there is something in the structure that supports these dreadful actions. This is important, because the tendency in organizations and in life is to blame individuals. A common approach when customer service is bad is to find the few people who are causing the problem and get rid of them. This seldom changes anything, and so leadership starts another round of ritual bloodletting, hoping to purge the organization of these toxins. They fail to see that bad customer service is embedded into how they do what they do.

If we understand the environment, we may be able to predict whether people will support us or not. Consider the following:

- How are people rewarded?
- How are they punished?
- What are people afraid of?
- What are their hopes?
- What structures and beliefs are in place that support the status quo?
- Because I may be part of this same environment, what impact does this environment have on my beliefs, thoughts, and actions?
- What impact does it have on how I choose to engage others?

Curt is director of programs in the adult education department of a university. The environment rewards people who go
along and don't make waves. People are afraid to speak up.
Meetings tend to be pretty dry affairs because no one wants to
take a risk. Within that context, Curt operates quite effectively.

He knows how the game is played. He never challenges his
boss (or anyone in authority) publicly. In fact, he suggests, offers,
builds on, and seldom confronts. It's slower and sometimes more
frustrating, but he gets things done. I've seen others just give up,
as if the environment wouldn't allow them to take any initiative.
One major difference between Curt and some of his colleagues is
that he understands the ground he is walking on and comes prepared. In similar environments, I have seen people lose their
ability to influence because they failed to read the signs and
forged ahead with their grand plans, only to be stopped dramatically. It is almost as if the organization itself had put up a sign
that read: Stop right there. You're not playing by the right rules.

The Impact of Beliefs on Relationships

Believing is seeing. Our beliefs limit our ability to take in what's
in front of us. In *The Republic*, Plato used the analogy of the cave.
Imagine people shackled to the wall of a cave; the only things
they can see are the shadows on the wall made by the firelight.
For them, that is reality. If these people were freed to walk out
into the sun, that world would seem unreal and unnatural.

We create our own images on cave walls. These pictures
come from our culture, people who are like us, families, school,
church, and media. These pictures allow us to get through the
day. There is nothing wrong with these pictures, except when
they limit our ability to see that other people may have different pictures. These different pictures on the wall can have a real
impact on our ability to make contact with other people. And
contact is vital if I want to influence you.

One way to begin to examine beliefs is to pay attention to
where we bump up against things that we think are wrong
with the other person. As we notice ourselves thinking, "How
could she say something like that?" or "That's the wrong way
to do that," we have an opportunity to dig beneath the surface
and ask ourselves what prompts those beliefs. For example,
I grew up in a small town in Ohio, and I believe people should
first connect with one another by being courteous. I have a
colleague from France who believes connection should come

Here are some questions about surface beliefs that can come into play when we are trying to influence someone:

- What are my assumptions about how people should act when they hear a new idea?
- How should people handle disagreements?
- How should people talk with one another?

from conflict. She believes that disagreement is a great starting point. Neither of us has a lock on the truth, but we run the risk of acting like we do. And that can create a problem. Instead of listening to each other's ideas, we run the risk of allowing the static of "how dare he/she say that" to get in the way.

Consider your responses in relation to the person you want to influence. In what ways is he or she different or similar? Especially note the differences, because that's where our belief that our pictures are right can get in the way.

When a major problem occurred on *Star Trek Voyager*, one of the characters said, "There is nothing wrong with me. There must be a mistake in the universe." Reflecting on our beliefs will allow us to break somewhat free of the egocentric trap that we are right and the universe is sorely lacking.

GOING FORWARD

In *Cat Ballou*, the classic parody of cowboy movies, Lee Marvin roars into a room bellowing and cursing. He then stops and notices that the room is full of people gathered around a casket topped with candles. He looks around, takes in the scene, walks over to the casket, sings "Happy Birthday," and blows out the candles. Just because there are candles doesn't guarantee that a birthday party is going on. Considering the context can only be a helpful tool if we pay attention.

In all the chapters so far, you've been getting ready to engage the other person. The next chapter, "Avoid Knee-Jerk Reactions," throws you into the center of the action.

AN ASSESSMENT: EXPLORING MY BELIEFS

- When I present an idea to _____, what do I believe the response should be if he/she likes the idea?
- What about when I present an idea that he/she is indifferent to?
- What if this person hates the idea?
- What assumptions do I make about this person when he/she follows my "rules" of engagement?
- What assumptions do I make about this person when he/she plays by a different set of rules?
- How do my own rules of conduct limit or enhance my ability to stay engaged with this person in an I/You manner?

These beliefs will have an impact on how you engage someone else. They can enhance or limit your ability to make a strong connection with the people you want to influence. Identifying your own attitudes and assumptions and keeping them in mind may help you see where you are strong or weak in helping the other person understand and react favorably to your idea, or in building their trust and confidence in you.

CHAPTER 6

Avoid Knee-Jerk Reactions

Where there's a will, there's a won't.

— Ambrose Bierce

Former U.S. Senator George Mitchell was chosen by the British and Irish governments to be chairman of the plenary sessions of the Northern Ireland peace accords. Of the nine parties involved in the talks, only seven agreed with his appointment. Opponents felt it was "the foisting upon them of an unelected chairman by 'despotic' governments." For two days, Mitchell and his staff had to sit across the hall and listen while his role was discussed. He called it a strange experience. Later he said, "The peace process is more important than my feelings . . . privately, my two colleagues and I were apprehensive. . . . It was humiliating, especially for me, but there was no realistic alternative, so we stayed and listened, joking among ourselves about our plight to keep our spirits up."

Finally, Senator Mitchell was allowed to enter the conference room. As he walked into the room, Dr. Ian Paisley, leader of the Democratic Unionist Party, said, "No." And he continued loudly, "No! No! No!"

"Before I could say or do anything, Paisley launched a blistering attack on the governments for 'imposing' me as chairman," Mitchell recalls. Paisley and his delegates left the room, and others immediately joined the walkout.

The remaining delegates watched Mitchell to see whether he was intimidated by the controversy. Mitchell says, "Realizing what was a stake, I tried to remain calm, to avoid betraying the swirling doubts I felt." He proceeded to make an opening statement, reminding delegates of the importance of the peace talks. He pledged to act in a fair and impartial manner. "I couldn't tell what effect my remarks had on those listening, but they helped me to calm down and gave me a few minutes to establish myself."[1]

Mitchell did something that is extremely difficult to do. He avoided knee-jerk reactions even in the face of continuous "humiliating" pressure. In Mitchell's case, had he responded defensively, his assignment might have ended before it began.

WHAT CAUSES KNEE-JERK REACTIONS

Knee-jerk reactions are our quick defenses against anything that we believe might harm us. Our brains detect danger before awareness kicks in.[2] Just recall Darwin's reaction when the puff adder struck at him. Sometimes our emotional brain picks up signals that are simply unavailable to the conscious mind.[3] Knee-jerk reactions can save our lives — and they can get us into trouble when the amygdala's hair trigger fires at times when we wish it wouldn't. We can say or do things that we may regret just moments later.

Our own Level 2 or Level 3 resistance to the other person is the primary reason why our knees start to jerk.

Emotions bump more mundane thoughts from our minds. For instance, when a rat sees a cat, it does not notice heat applied to its tail.[4] Just as our idea may bump another person into a Level 2 I-Don't-*Like*-It reaction, that person's response to us may drop us into a knee-jerk response. And when that occurs, our ability to pay attention to other parts of the conversation may diminish or vanish completely.

Knee-jerk reactions occur as we engage another person, but they also can occur in anticipation of something happening. We seem to be the only species that has the capacity to anticipate the future. With that comes hope, but also fear of what the future might hold. We can work ourselves into a lather as we create scenarios in our minds about what *might* happen. While these stories may protect us from danger, they also can provide such a strong shield that we miss seeing the other person. We react to slights that have little (or no) basis in reality.

The preparation that comes from considering the context can help us to do a reality check as we examine what we know about ourselves, the other person, and the situation. A clear intent that includes the other person in our thinking can help us stay focused, even in the midst of a huge display of amygdala fireworks. But something happens in that moment of engagement that can throw us off our game. The other person says something so surprising that we react before we know what hit us — or them. That's why it is important to understand our own triggers.

WHAT HOOKS US

Because people are different, what triggers you may hold no charge for me. A car cuts you off on a major highway and you think, "Wow, I'm so glad I could allow him to move ahead of me. He must be in an awfully big hurry." Not me. I have been known to roll down the window and shout blistering phrases that can't be printed here.

Knowing what is likely to trigger these reactions can help us anticipate them, and we can begin to view the triggers in a different light when they do occur. There actually have been times when drivers have cut me off and I just smiled and slowed down enough to allow the car to enter my lane safely. During those fleeting moments, I realized that it is possible to change my own behavior in tense situations.

Here are some ways we can get hooked:

- **Someone attacks our intelligence.** Any statement that feels like an attack aimed directly at us can make our knees start jerking. For some, "You're an idiot" elicits a Vesuvian reaction, whereas "Where'd you learn business? From a matchbook-cover correspondence course?" may be all it takes to launch someone else into a knee-jerk reaction.
- **Someone attacks our idea.** Something like "That's got to be the dumbest idea I've ever heard" may set us off. Sometimes we love our idea so much and are so fearful that others won't see its brilliance that even simple questions of clarification can seem like attacks.

- **Someone attacks our integrity.** "You're supporting that policy and you call yourself a decent person? I'd be ashamed if I were you."
- **Someone attacks our values and beliefs.** "How could anyone believe something like that?"
- **Someone attacks our group.** This is a Level 3 blanket statement about some group you are part of. "You people always say . . ." For starters, this could refer to your race, gender, ethnicity, role in the organization, sexual orientation — but this is a long list.
- **Someone uses their status against us.** The other person uses his or her relative higher status to make us feel smaller. "When you get to be my age, you'll understand." This may play out as condescension. The person talks down at us as if we couldn't possibly be taken seriously.
- **Someone ignores us or our idea.** The other person simply will not pay attention to us. He or she doesn't return calls or honor appointments.
- **Someone questions our competence.** The person attempts to lower our status by implying, "What makes you think you're qualified to do that?"
- **Someone makes us fear a loss of honor or reputation.** More homicides are committed over the loss of honor than any other reason. This reaction isn't limited to young men hanging out in clubs. In 1804, the vice-president of the United States, Aaron Burr, killed Alexander Hamilton, a founding father and author of *The Federalist Papers*, in a duel.
- **We want to win at all costs.** For some, the trigger may be perceived competition. When this kicks in, we forget about our original intent and focus on winning. In 1973, Barry Diller, the vice-president of primetime programming for ABC, bid $3.3 million for rights to a single showing of *The Poseidon Adventure*. This was $1 million over what they could expect to earn from the sale of ads. Robert Wood, who was president of CBS television, said, "We were very rational at the start. . . . But then the bidding started . . . and the fever of the thing caught us. Like a guy who had lost his mind, I kept bidding. . . . There came a moment when I said to myself, 'Good grief, if I get it, what the heck am I going to do with it?' When ABC finally topped me, my main feeling was relief."[5]

THE TYPES OF KNEE-JERK REACTIONS

Early twentieth century psychoanalyst Karen Horney identified three major ways in which we handle anxiety: We can
move against, move toward, or move away from the other person. Her model serves well to look at how we handle perceived
attacks to our ideas.

Move Against: I/you

To move against is to attack. It is the fight part of fight-flight.
In our quick reaction, we act as if fighting is the only way to
get out of this perilous situation. The goal is to win or to beat
the other person. We place protection of ourselves and our
idea over the relationship. I/You is destroyed. Our stance
becomes capital I over a small you: I/you.

Here are some of the ways it plays out:

- **You threaten.** "You'll go along with this idea — or
  else." Leaders talking about change in the workplace
  often use war metaphors to describe the situation. They
  will "shoot the stragglers" and "take no prisoners."
- **You use force of reason.** This is a gentler form of moving
  against, but it is an attack just the same. You assume you
  can convince the person to go along if you only explain
  your idea repeatedly. You will prevail through the sheer
  force of your arguments based on crystalline logic.
- **You kill the messenger.** In order to move ahead, you
  destroy the person or group that has the audacity to
  question your plans. Your methods may be a bit more
  humane than the ancient Romans, who literally killed
  messengers who brought bad news — but destroy them
  you do. One way to figuratively kill a messenger is to
  seek revenge later.
- **You ignore the opposition.** You so believe you are right
  that you simply don't have time for it. You see the
  resistance, but disregard it. You may ignore opposition
  because you think you can afford to. You move ahead
  like a bulldozer, pushing aside anything or anybody that
  gets in the way.

Moving against often appears in how we speak and carry
ourselves. Our voices may become more forceful. Our bodies

tense. People see our veins throbbing. We point, using our index finger as a saber. Our eyes narrow and focus intently on the other person as if we could burrow through them with a laser ray.

Moving against creates a contest with a winner and a loser.

Move Toward: i/YOU

When we move toward, we are so concerned about losing the relationship that we give up our own idea and focus exclusively on saving the relationship. The You in I/You takes precedence over the I. Moving too far in the direction of You can throw us off balance. We pay too much attention to our need to maintain the relationship and forget our goal. In this case our I is minimized: little i, capital YOU.

Here's what it can look like:

- **You capitulate.** You give in to others, even when you don't agree. Because you are moving toward the other person, you capitulate in order to maintain contact. You give in so you don't risk losing the relationship. You may not recognize that you have given in until after the fact. A day later you may think to yourself, "How could I have agreed to do that?"
- **You make deals.** This is similar to capitulation, but in this variation you look for ways to turn this into a tit-for-tat exchange: "I'll give you this if you'll give me that." Reciprocity is an important social skill. Doing favors and having them done for us are an important part of life. And these give-and-take exchanges work fine when the stakes are small. But as a knee-jerk reaction, you can find yourself making deals you later regret.
- **You lessen the impact.** You may attempt to lessen the impact of the idea as you pull away: "You didn't think I was serious about that bone-headed idea, did you? You know me better than that. Come on, I was kidding."

Move Away: i/you

When we move away, we pull back from the relationship itself. We give up our idea and, at least temporarily, our connection to the other person. We pull away for safety. We give up the I, the You, and the It. Everything is small case: i/you.

This appears in the following ways:

- **You give in too soon.** You quit before you know how strong the opposition is — is it mild resistance or major? You'll never know because you backed out before you could find out. This occurs because the foe seems too formidable, and you believe you are too weak.
- **You go into a protective shell.** Your rational thoughts are clouded by the emotions of the moment, and you create a cocoon for yourself. Even though you may stay in the room, only a small part of you is still trying to talk with the other person.
- **You deflect.** You may change the subject in an attempt to get the attention off you and your idea. Some of us use humor to deflect attention away from whatever is triggering it. Like the person who shouts, "Look over there!" we try to have everyone focus on some-thing else.

The Frozen State

There is one other way people respond to a threat from some-one else: They freeze. They might like to move against, move away, or move toward, but they can't; they are frozen. Once they move out of the frozen state, they can move toward, against, or away from the other person, but they still are react-ing defensively to the situation.

KNOWING THE CONSEQUENCES

Awareness marks the difference between a knee-jerk reaction and a strategic response to a situation. If I choose to move away with awareness, then I am mindful of the consequences of my action. So I may make a choice to move away, knowing that the strategy could work against my intention. Awareness of my action and of how the other person responds allows me to refine or change my tactic based on feedback. When I move away in a knee-jerk reaction, I miss all of those signals. It is only later that I realize the potential consequences, and then it may be harder to reestablish contact. Of course, this same spilt between mindfulness and knee-jerk *mindlessness* occurs when we move against or move toward as well.

LIVING IN THE WORLD OF
LEVEL 3 RESISTANCE

There are times when we may find ourselves living in a Level 3 environment of resistance. It is important to recognize what this world looks like or you run the risk of going crazy with your knee jerking day and night.

Everything seems skewed in a Level 3 world. As you walk around this carnival funhouse, your reflection looks odd in the mirror, everyone's voices are distorted, and you can't seem to get your footing. Nothing is quite right. In this world, a small slight becomes a betrayal. A forgotten promise becomes the symbol that nothing is right or ever will be right between you. It is as if everyone were dissecting each phrase to look for the real meaning behind every word you utter. You become wary of what you say and how you say it. Strategy wins out over intimacy. Conflicts that come up between you and another person get exaggerated way out of proportion. Everything feels bigger and weightier. You find yourself expending a significant amount of energy just getting through the day. It's like you can't go home from this twisted carnival.

When I am living in a world like this, I can easily feel like a victim and believe that "they" are the ones who made everything bad. If only they would change. If only they had the insight into themselves and the situation that I have, this would be a great place to be. If they'd only listen to me, get over whatever's bothering them, we could get back to work, and get things done.

Here's the bad news. Although we may feel like a victim in this tragedy, the truth is that most everyone feels like a victim. But more important, we are not anthropologists sitting on the fringes of this village noting the odd behavior of these strange people. We are part of the village, both perpetrator and victim.

The good news, of course, is that if we are part of it all — and are willing to admit it — we may be able to begin to change things. Level 3 resistance doesn't change in a day, and in the most severe situations, it won't even change in a lifetime, but perhaps we can make headway. I have seen people make a difference in the culture of their organizations. But it ain't easy, nor is it always successful.

And the *somewhat* good news: Even if we are powerless to change the overall Level 3 conditions, we may be able to make a difference in our little part of the world. I have worked with union stewards and managers who have found ways to work well together — and even enjoy each other's company — in spite of the strong animosity between the two sides. The danger is that, even when two people can create a peace and work together developing projects and new ideas, Level 3 is always in the air. A shift in senior management's position on benefits could cause your friend on the organized labor side of the business to pull back. In the world of Level 3, trust is difficult to build and easy to destroy.

Sometimes we can change some of the fundamental conditions that create Level 3, sometimes we can change those conditions in our personal relationships, and sometimes we may feel powerless to do anything. In the last instance, it may be time to leave. Aikido is a martial art that uses conflict as a way to work toward harmony. A black belt was showing me all the moves you could make on someone who was attacking you in a particular way. I asked, "But what if none of those techniques work?" He replied, "Then sometimes you've just got to get out of Dodge." (More about when to leave and when to stay in chapter 12.)

The Positive Side

All three reactions — move toward, move against, and move away — have their positive sides to be sure.

- We can move toward another in ways that call for joining, cooperation, and affection. The problem comes when moving toward turns into compliance.
- We can move against at times when others need to hear someone take a strong stand. The problem occurs when assertiveness turns to aggression.
- We can move away when the odds are too formidable and waiting for another day may be prudent. The problem occurs when people become detached and, as Horney suggests, "the universe votes for them."[6]

Unfortunately, little of the positive attributes of these styles is available to us when we are in full knee-jerk mode. It is difficult — sometimes impossible — to gain any of the potential from these if we are off balance.

Making Matters Worse

The more typical consequences of knee-jerk reactions are to make matters worse. This can occur in many ways.

Escalation

When knee jerk meets knee jerk, problems can escalate way out of control. During the Cuban Missile Crisis, when the Soviets decided to place their missiles in Cuba, senior U.S. officials were discussing implications if the United States were to invade Cuba in response and take out the missiles. According to Tom Blanton, director of the National Security Archive, leaders from past administrations were invited in to advise ExCom, the executive committee of the National Security Council.

During one of the meetings, former Secretary of State Dean Acheson wanted to make a point about the risk they were facing. He is supposed to have said, "Of course, we've got to take them out" (to "take out" means to destroy by force). Then someone asked him, "How would the Soviets respond to that?"

He responded, "I suppose they'd have to take out our missiles in Turkey." "Well, what would we do in response to that?"

Acheson replied, "Oh well, to support our NATO alliance and back up our ally, Turkey, we'd probably have to attack some of the Soviet missiles maybe in the Soviet Union."

"Well, what happens then?"

"Well, hopefully by then cooler heads would prevail."

Blanton says that Acheson led them through these exaggerated steps in order to show that cooler heads need to prevail at the beginning. Once a knee-jerk pattern begins, it is hard to stop it.[7]

Interrupting I/You Contact

A knee jerk is a signal that we are more concerned about our survival than we are about the relationship. Fear responses are a good thing. They can protect us from real danger. However, when these reactions are triggered by situations that are less than life-threatening, our amygdalas may be calibrated to respond a little too quickly. Moving against (*I/you*), moving toward (*i/YOU*), and moving away (*i/you*), all lack the grit necessary for a full I and You exchange.

Building Level 3 Animosity
People who rely on knee-jerk reactions as their common way of working with others invite opposition. This works against them as mistrust builds in others. Over time, relationships are severely damaged.

AVOIDING KNEE-JERK REACTIONS

There are ways to control our impulsive actions. Here are a few.

Focus on Your Intent
When knee jerks hit, it is easy to forget why we started talking in the first place. Suddenly, and without warning, we may forget our original intent — to engage the other person, paying attention to I and You — and we revert to an instinctive moving against, toward, or away reaction. A strong intention that we believe in deeply can help us stop reacting when we perceive a threat.

In 1959, James Lawson, an African-American divinity student at Vanderbilt University, was committed to pacifist teaching as a way to end racial injustice. He was as "absolutely clear in his mission" as he was of his own "vision of what America should be." During a four-month sit-in to try to integrate lunch counters in Nashville, student protesters endured ketchup being poured on them and lighted cigarettes placed against their necks. As minister C. T. Vivian knelt in prayer, a white boy punched him. One of the students raised his fists to retaliate. Vivian called to mind Lawson's non-violent teaching and said, "Put your hands in your pockets." The protester obeyed.[8]

Vivian's intent was clear — to protest non-violently — and he was so committed to this course of action that even physical abuse did not deter him. I suspect that in his work with Lawson, he learned a considerable amount about the context as well, so that the abuse was not a surprise. Intent combined with a deep knowledge of the context can help us avoid reflex actions that take us away from our goals.

Know Your Triggers
Recall the list earlier in this chapter of things that could trigger a knee-jerk reaction. It's important to know what might set

you off in specific situations. What are the things that a particular person could say or do that would cause *your* knees to jerk? Perhaps it is a phrase or the way someone speaks to you. Two different people can have dramatically different reactions to the same words.

Practice

Practice may not make perfect, but it sure can help. Research shows that exposure to something can help us build acceptance of it.[9] Exposure to triggers that set us off can help dispel some of the power they may hold over us.

Use a "Mouth Brace"

Some who suffer from migraine headaches use a simple mouth brace. When you put it in your mouth, it relaxes the jaw muscles, relieving stress and reducing the intensity of the migraine headache (and sometimes eliminating it altogether). Using this as an analogy, you might consider something similar — something that would remind you to relax or take a breath. Sometimes I draw a simple picture in the top corner of my notepad: a small circle with three dots in it. This represents a connect-the-dots picture with too few dots to make much sense yet. It is a reminder that I am there to learn something from the other person. It helps me keep my mouth shut when I really should be listening and learning.

Wait for a Better Time

Sometimes the timing is wrong for us to engage another person. We can already feel the tension building in anticipation of talking with this person. In this instance, moving away might be a great choice. Once we are a bit calmer, we may be freer to engage him or her more openly.

One way to tell when the timing is wrong is to listen to the dialogue we are carrying on in our heads. If we are plotting strategy and coming up with ways we are going to slam the person, put him in his place, make him feel rotten, we may already be in full knee jerk. As good as saying these things may feel in the short term, we must ask ourselves, "Will these actions on my part move me closer to my goal?"

WAYS TO STOP MID-JERK

While it is best to avoid knee-jerk reactions before they occur, sometimes we can't. The surprise or intensity is so great that the situation gets the better of us and we kick into full jerk before we know what hit us or them. These days, my worst knee-jerk reactions often come in moments when I don't expect anything to go wrong. For instance, I may call my bank with a question about my account. Then I am shuttled from person to person, with no one seeming to care or be able to address the problem. What seemed like a simple call has turned into an epic encounter. And each time I am put on hold, my patience drains just a bit more. In those moments, I may react to the next person in the chain without thinking.

All is not lost. We can often turn things around if we catch ourselves and shift attention back to our original goal, which, in my case, was to get an answer to my question.

Catch Yourself

Pay attention to your own unique blend of signals that let you know you have moved into knee-jerk range, such as:

- **Your words.** Note the words you use when you are in a knee-jerk response. They often differ from day-to-day speech. They may be stronger or weaker. They may be sarcastic or kind. They may attack, be overly rational and legalistic, or be overly mild. There is no one-size-fits-all pattern. You must identify your own unique patterns.
- **Muscle tension.** Muscles react instantly, sometimes well before the conscious mind has had a chance to figure out what is going on. If we are attentive to those shifts and note where tension is growing in our bodies, we may be able to stop a knee jerk. These physical signals — a furrowed brow, muscles in the shoulder or neck beginning to tighten, our hands held differently than usual, or our jaw beginning to clench — can be early warning signs that trouble is on the way.
- **Pulse.** It usually goes up. If you are someone who can pick up on this signal, use this data.

- **The words the other person uses.** Know the words that trigger knee-jerk responses in you.

Shift Attention

When you notice that you have moved into a knee-jerk reaction, you now have options:

- **Shift to I/You.** This shift in intention from I/It to I/You is by far the most important and reliable tool. When we are in a knee-jerk mode, we lose the I/You relationship. Our attention may turn to all I: "I've got to get out of here" (move away). It may turn to all It: "I've got to get the idea sold no matter what" (move against). And it may result in giving up our I and It and going too far into the You portion of the equation: "I've got to maintain this relationship at all costs" (move toward).

  Theater director Keith Johnstone believes that stage fright occurs when we lose contact with our scene partner and focus too much on ourselves ("Will I remember my lines?" "How am I doing?" "She's getting more laughs than I am tonight.").[10] When we are nervous, we risk paying attention to our own nervousness, instead of to the work we are doing.

  Johnstone suggests shifting the attention back to the relationship, since that's the reason you are there in the first place. That simple advice has helped me countless times in meetings with clients. Just when I start to get nervous and feel my favorite knee jerk — using logic and details — kick in, I remember his advice and shift the focus to the relationship.

  This shift is in keeping with the spirit of I/You. Refocusing on I/You — on the importance of the relationship — is the best antidote to automatic knee-jerk reactions.
- **Take a break.** Sometimes it is as if we are listening to a play in which we already know the outcome. We listen to a tape reciting our lines, knowing that the outcome will be tragic. But we feel trapped. We are in the middle of this terrible play, and there are still three acts to go.

STOPPING MID-JERK

1. Identify what triggers knee-jerk reactions in you from a particular person who is important to you.
2. How do you react?
3. What do you notice just as this reaction kicks in (e.g., muscles tensing, pulse rate increasing, voice rising in volume or pitch)?
4. What have you done in other situations to stop yourself from continuing with a knee-jerk reaction?
5. How can you support yourself when you meet with this person again?

In order to make a shift to I/You, you may need to take a break. Sometimes a momentary break in the action can allow you to regain your balance and remember your intention. If possible, leave the room. Or get up and walk across the room and get something to drink. Do anything to shift your own attention away from the situation for a moment. This shift may occur while someone else is talking during a meeting, giving you a brief respite. It may come from simply taking a few deep breaths.

Groucho Marx was famous for his quick ad-libs to guests on the game show "You Bet Your Life." People knew the character he had created so well that just a wiggle of the cigar could get a laugh. But it served another purpose as well. A puff on the cigar bought him just an extra moment to think up his response.[11] I'm not suggesting that you take up smoking, but you might find some small thing that serves the same function as Groucho's cigar.

- **Admit what's happening to you.** It's amazing what the truth can do: "I just realized that I've been doing all the talking. And the reason I came here was to find out what you thought of the idea." "Excuse me, I'm getting a bit carried away. I apologize. I didn't mean to attack

your ideas. Obviously, I believe in the idea I'm presenting, so why don't I shut up for a few minutes and listen
to what you think?"

Chapter 10, "Stay Calm to Stay Engaged," covers
other ways to help you avoid knee-jerk reactions.

HOW TO START

Begin small, in seemingly insignificant situations, and just
notice what's going on. With forgiveness toward yourself in
your heart, begin to notice when you feel yourself reacting in a
knee-jerk manner. Ask yourself, "Am I moving toward, against,
or away? What impact is that having? Is it getting me closer to
my goals or moving me further from them? Is this reaction
building a bridge with the other person or destroying its
underpinnings?"

Before we can change our behavior, we must first fully grasp
what we are doing today. If we notice what we are doing with
harsh judgment, we'll have difficulty seeing ourselves clearly
enough to change. In a way, we need to extend the humanity
of I/You to ourselves. Instead of creating an idealized "It" that
we must achieve by giving up bad habits, we could try to be
more accepting of what we are doing now.

It may help to remember that knee jerks are our own
attempts to protect ourselves from harm — and that's a good
thing. We developed these automatic responses over time for
good reasons. It's not that they are bad, but simply that in some
cases they may be over-used or their utility has run its course.

The principles of engagement are not steps. In fact, four of
them — Avoid Knee-Jerk Reactions, Pay Attention, Explore
Deeply, and Find Ways to Connect — are tightly linked. They
move back and forth like a fine dance. Paying attention can
show us tension in the other person or reveal that our own
knee is starting to jerk. Paying attention tells us that it is time
to explore differences. As we explore differences, we must
be mindful of knee jerks just waiting to kick. We can't pay
attention once and then think we've completed that step and
move on. We need to pay attention throughout the process.
We need to avoid knee-jerk reactions throughout as well. And we
need to explore differences whenever they occur.

CHAPTER 7

Pay Attention

If other people are going to talk, conversation becomes impossible.
— James McNeill Whistler

Terry Anderson was a hostage in Lebanon for over seven years. He was often in extremely cramped quarters with others. One day a new hostage arrived, whom Anderson refers to as TW. Anderson said that the new hostage "cannot seem to understand that there are things he does that drive the rest of us crazy, especially Tom, whose mattress is right next to him, just inches away. TW is not very observant, or very good at reading moods. Often, each of us wants to be alone and undisturbed with our thoughts. . . . John and I have learned to read those signs in each other, and heed them. TW wants to talk all the time, no matter what we want."

It gets worse. "When he does engage in conversation, he has the large man's habit of moving in close, until he looms over you. I tried the other day to ask him not to do that . . . he just couldn't understand."[1]

THE COST OF MISSED SIGNALS

How can we influence others if we can't pick up their signals? Do they understand? How are they reacting? Do they trust us? In Terry Anderson's story, TW couldn't even pick up direct feedback. Being oblivious to another person suggests that I — my thoughts, my needs, my whatever — am far more important than whatever you have in mind. When this occurs, I run the risk of missing your excitement, joy, anger, confusion, or dismay. I am so wrapped up in me or my idea — my I or It — that I miss your reactions.

When we miss cues, we lose the opportunity to make I/You contact. Almost by default, we turn the other person into an It. BJ paid attention to his own needs and turned the other hostages into Its. Even after feedback, he still seemed unable to understand the impact he was having on others.

When we want someone to be excited about our idea, we need to be attentive to more than the idea. We must pay attention to what's going on in the relationship between us. Is the other person interested? Indifferent? Angry? We can only tell if we pay attention.

Here's the dilemma. Most of us think we are doing just fine. In one study, men were asked to rate their ability to get along with others. Everyone put himself in the upper half of the population. And 60 percent rated themselves in the upper 10 percent. Twenty-five percent put themselves in the top 1 percent. (Similar delusions occurred when men were asked about their leadership and athletic ability.)[2] Just because the study was conducted on men doesn't automatically absolve women of this trait to be wildly optimistic about themselves. Daniel Goleman, author of *Emotional Intelligence*, states that generally people are not very good at determining their own emotional intelligence.[3] The ability to pay attention to our idea and the relationship simultaneously lies at the core of the six principles covered in this book.

INTENTION IS KEY

Becoming better at paying attention to the impact we are having has little to do with skills and a lot to do with having a clear intention. You could learn the skills of active listening: You could paraphrase, summarize, and reflect the emotional content of what the other person is saying — and still not be paying attention. All those listening skills are fine, of course, but they don't get at the heart of the issue, which is, "Do I care about what the other person has to say?"

Carl Rogers wrote that "the major barrier to interpersonal communication is our very natural tendency to judge, to evaluate, to approve or disapprove the statement of the other

person."[4] Even though Rogers is credited with showing thera-
pists and people in general the importance of reflective listening, he seems to suggest that this natural tendency to judge —
in other words, our implicit intention — gets in the way.

Without a clear intention, techniques will break down when
put to a test. During an intensive eight-week management training program, Javier gave a presentation that was poorly received.
Some in the audience were strong in their criticisms. On reading
the evaluations, the rest of us on Javier's team learned that people were angry at what he had said. We suggested that he explore
the issue with the group the next morning. He agreed.

The next morning, Javier stood in front of the group and acknowledged what he had read in the evaluations. He asked people to elaborate on what they had written. So far, so good.
People began to make a few critical comments, and that was all
Javier could take. He began justifying the way he had presented
material the day before and kept talking for almost thirty minutes. When the team discussed this later, Javier believed he had
been responsive and open to their criticism. His knee-jerk reaction of explaining his thinking ad nauseum with the group and
with his colleagues blocked his ability to pay attention.

His influence on the team and with participants began to
diminish. People started to tune him out when he went into
one of his orations. Sadly, he never seemed to be aware of this,
and consequently, he couldn't see that he did have choices in
the way he engaged us. He was a bright guy and had a lot to
contribute, but his influence was never as great as it might
have been.

SHIFT TO I/YOU

In my experience, customer service departments often don't
want to hear what the customer has to say. Complaints and
suggestions are treated with scripted replies, "We're sorry that
your toaster exploded. We at Allied Toasters are committed to
offering you the finest in toaster technology." You can almost hear the pages turning quickly in the service manual as
the customer service rep searches for the listing: Toasters,
Exploding. In these instances, the customer has become an It.

We have a choice. We can treat people like objects and act
like we are paying attention or we can really pay attention. If

our goal is to focus on our idea — and stay engaged with the other person — then there really is no choice. We've got to see the human behind the words. We can't afford to use our scripted replies.

If we really care about what the customer has to say — we've got to pay attention. And we've got to pay attention to more than just the words. The words people use only tell us part of the story, and sometimes the words mask the true intent. That's why listening beyond the words is so important. Listening beyond the words is especially important in the workplace, where people are trained to speak without saying what's really on their minds.

WAYS TO PAY ATTENTION

Here are some ways to listen that support your intention of an I/You relationship.

Listen to Be Changed

The director and actor Andre Gregory said, "As an actor, I have great trouble with [listening]. In life, I'm a great listener. When I'm acting, I'm a very bad listener because I'm always so worried about my next response, or my cue."[5] That worry about the next line, or making sure we make it to where we need to be in time, gets in the way of listening. And yet, if we want to influence, that's exactly what we must be able to do.

The actor Alan Alda said, "Listening is being able to be changed by the other person. Not hearing them, not waiting for your cue, not waiting for them to stop so I can talk — it's letting them in."[6] Alda is speaking to a willingness to be influenced by the other person. I believe he is speaking about an I/You intention, whereby each person can be influenced by the other. All of us know how to listen; we've been doing it since we were very young. If we hold in mind our intent of being able to be changed by the other person, listening skills become secondary. Listening is really not a set of skills, but holding an intent to be willing to be changed. (However, if you'd like a reminder of some fundamental listening skills, visit www.beyondresistance.com for an article I wrote on listening. You can access it at no charge.)

If we are willing to be changed by the other person, then it is almost impossible to influence in a way that puts our wishes over theirs. If we listen with the willingness to be influenced, we are open to other possibilities: new ideas and modifications to our original thoughts. And we may even be open to being wrong.

Leaning In and Leaning Away

If we did no more than pay attention to whether the other person is leaning in or leaning away from

Listening with a *willingness to be changed* does not suggest that we roll over and give in. However, it does suggest that we hold the I and the You in equal regard. I keep my idea in mind while, at the same time, I take in what you have to say in a way that allows me to be influenced.

us, it could provide invaluable information about his or her interest in our idea or in us. When we are trying to influence another person, just about everything we do brings us closer together or moves us apart: our tone of voice, pace, gestures — every phrase and sentence counts in this subtle dance. You may say or do something that pushes the other person back. If you are oblivious to this, you push him even farther back.

In a not-so-subtle example, think of a time when you've been stuck talking with someone who had truly bad breath. He leans in and you lean back just an inch. That doesn't provide relief, so you take a step back. He steps forward, you bump against the punch bowl, laugh nervously, and step to the side. A videotape would reveal an elaborate and ungraceful waltz as the two of you glide across the room with the Breathman leading and you reacting to his every move.

But often these leaning in and leaning away movements can be extremely subtle and very hard to see. In my experience, the people who are most successful in building excitement for their ideas can read and respond to these tiny signals moment to moment. They would notice when you moved your head back or inadvertently tapped the punch bowl ever so gently. They would stop the dance well before it was underway.

In most conversations we move back and forth. I say something that pulls you closer, you respond in kind. Inadvertently, I do something that causes you to take a step back. If I am paying attention, I can move with you and try to reconnect. But if I am oblivious, like the Breathman, I will push you farther and farther away.

As I write the first draft of this chapter, Chris is making a presentation to his colleagues about a new project. (The fact that I am working on a book while this is going on should be a tip-off that Chris is not paying attention to signals about the level of excitement I have for his ideas.) Many in the group seem to be doing other work. Some leave to make calls. Some work on their personal organizers. Maybe half the group is looking at Chris while he talks. He seems very interested in the idea he is presenting, but apparently is unaware of the impact he is having on the group he wants to influence. When the lights come up, he receives polite applause but no commitment from anyone to do anything.

It is common to pay attention to just a limited part of what is occurring between another person and ourselves. We need to pay attention to more than the words; we need to be attentive to their emotional reactions and issues of trust as well.

If Chris had shifted his attention to his audience, thinking to himself, "I want to connect with them. I want them to become as excited as I am about this idea," he could have covered the same content, but he would have been able to engage us in a different way. He would have noticed me writing, others leaving the room, and the polite, but glazed, looks.

Imagine if Chris had noticed that people were fidgeting. He could have stopped, smiled, and joked, "You don't like this very much, do you?" People might have laughed nervously and reluctantly admitted that they agreed with him. He might then have asked what they didn't like about the project. This could have begun a rich and spirited conversation.

We all have the capacity to take on this other way of working — but it may seem unnatural, even bizarre. In fact, we all may have many options available if we but pay attention. For instance, if Chris had been paying attention, he could have continued to talk at the group. He could have modified his message. He could have quit talking. He could have raised his voice. But he couldn't consider even a single option if he wasn't paying attention.

Acting with awareness gives us options. When Chris saw people in the group fidgeting and not paying attention, he could have assumed that this was a sign that people were restless and uncomfortable with the idea. He could have decided to check this assumption.

As you present your idea, pay attention to how others are reacting to you and to the idea itself. Also, pay attention to how you respond to other people and to your own excitement about the idea. Too often, we become so enamored with "making the sale" that we lose contact with everything else, including the other person. That can be dangerous.

If we want to stay excited about our idea and stay engaged with the other person, then we must pay attention to the idea and to the person simultaneously.

Act in the Moment

Theater improv teaches actors not to plan ahead but to respond in the moment to whatever they are offered. This is a great way to learn to pay attention in a way that allows you to be influenced by the other person.

Imagine an improv in which the director tells the actors they are two people trapped on a desert island. The scene begins. Are you friends, strangers, enemies? No one knows

SIGNALS YOU'RE NOT PAYING ATTENTION IN THE MOMENT

- You're paying more attention to making your point than you are to what's occurring between you.
- You're preparing arguments and counterpoints while the other person is talking.
- You're already anticipating the outcome of this meeting.
- You're distracted by something else.
- You're already plotting what you'll do after this meeting.
- You're judging your own performance and allowing that to distract you.

until one of you speaks and makes something up. Imagine your partner says, "You idiot! Why did I ever marry you?" Suddenly, a world is created. You are married and your spouse is very angry. (Probably Level 3.) Now you've got something to play with. If you are paying attention, you can respond to what you've just been given. If not, you'll take the scene in another direction.

At a performance by a nationally known improv troop, one actor was very clever and funny. In scenes she often responded with quick, witty comments. The audience enjoyed these moments, but often her comments took the life out of the scenes. Few scenes were able to develop because she kept cutting across any ideas that were building up any head of steam. She did nothing to build on what her partners had given her. You could see the others try hard to reshape the scene to include what she had just said, but her wit kept them off balance.

Yes, she acted in the moment, but she used the ideas of others as a launching pad for her own wit. She failed to pay attention in a way that allowed scenes to develop. With an I/You intent, she could have listened in ways that built on the previous lines. She wouldn't always get the laughs, but she would help create the conditions for the laughs to occur. She wasn't using I/You, and maybe not even I/It, she seemed to be most interested in I/I/I/I.

This same cleverness occurs in meetings every day. Just as a few people start to become interested in something, Rocko cuts across with his very own idea. He only pays attention to what's important to him and fails to build on or even comment on the comments of others. The Rockos of the world (and he's got a lot of relatives roaming the halls of organizations) sap the life out of meetings.

Paying attention closely in a meeting (or in a scene) can be helpful in knowing what to say next. Rather than preparing what you are going to say while the other person is speaking, you might try actually listening and then responding to what you just heard.

Imagine you want a colleague to accept your priorities on next year's budget. Of course, you think about how you are going to present the idea, but once the two of you meet, you stay open to how she reacts. If she is excited, you build on that. If she seems quizzical, you respond appropriately. If she seems distracted, you consider meeting at another time. If she seems upset by the idea, you explore. These options are only available if you remain open to the person in front of you.

You can only plan ahead with regard to the It of your presentation — its content and style. You cannot plan ahead for how the relationship will play. The You will need to unfold as the two of you work together.

In Neil Simon's play *Brighton Beach Memoirs*, the main character walks to the front of the stage, puts down a bag of groceries he was bringing home to his mother, and talks to the audience about life. During one performance in Washington, D.C., a teenaged Matthew Broderick accidentally kicked the bag into the orchestra pit. He looked at the bag and then at the audience and said, "My Mom is going to be really mad at me." The audience laughed and he continued with the scene. He could react quickly because he was open to whatever happened.

Staying open to what's in front of you can allow you to see when to suggest something or move forward. Gitta Sereny wrote a landmark biography of Albert Speer, who was Minister of Armaments in the Third Reich and a member of Hitler's inner circle. On the rare occasions in her interviews with Speer when conversation veered toward "difficult topics," she says that Speer delivered responses that were "deliberately calculated to deflect attention from matters he didn't want to — or couldn't — talk about." So Sereny listened — and waited for fleeting moments when Speer's defenses broke. "There were only a few such moments of transformation, but in each case I was suddenly keenly and somewhat frighteningly aware — I can still feel my stomach knotting — of the authority coiled inside this man, which manifestly suppressed with constant deliberate effort, only burst out at moments of disappointment, intense irritation or weary anger."[7]

PAYING ATTENTION AFTER THE CONVERSATION

Brenda serves on the board of her church. She proposed some changes in how they could strengthen outreach to the community. The board approved the ideas and then nothing happened.

It's important to keep our eyes, ears, and guts open after the initial contact. We may miss signals when we meet, or others may be adept at masking their true thoughts and feelings. Perhaps your contact has been over the phone or through e-mail, where many of these cues are hard (and sometimes impossible) to read.

By paying attention, even after the meeting, Brenda can still go back to the board and explore these so-called decisions again. Here are a few things that might signal that people aren't as interested in this idea as you are:

- **No action.** It seemed that you had an agreement, but nothing has happened.
- **Malicious compliance.** A charismatic company president was a champion of quality improvement. Nobody could say no to his enthusiastic exhortations. Even when he came around to their work areas and asked about it, all people could say was, "It's going well." He told me that it took him months to realize that all he was getting was malicious compliance. People were doing just enough and saying just the right words to keep him off their backs or not hurt his feelings.
- **Sabotage.** The other person works against your efforts in some underhanded way.
- **Erosion in the relationship.** The person is going ahead with your idea, but things ain't what they used to be between you. You find that it's difficult to reach agreement on other issues. Or perhaps you find that the former ease in your relationship is starting to strain.

BECOMING MORE ADEPT AT PAYING ATTENTION

How do you get better at paying attention? It's actually quite simple: Pay attention to paying attention. In other words, don't practice diligently, just notice what you do. Timothy Gallwey revolutionized tennis instruction by suggesting that people simply notice what they are doing with no attempt to change it. He calls it the art of relaxed concentration. Once you focus on what you believe might need improvement, simply notice this action without judgment. A much more typical response to learning is to be highly judgmental about our performance. This can get in the way of learning, Gallwey says.

> It is the initial act of judgment which provokes the thinking process. First the player's mind judges one of his shots as bad or good. If he judges it as bad, he begins thinking about what was wrong with it. Then he tells himself how to correct it. Then he *tries* hard, giving himself instructions as he does so. . . . Obviously, the mind is anything but still and the body is tight with trying . . . the player's muscles tighten when they need to be loose, strokes become awkward and less fluid, and negative evaluations are likely to continue with growing intensity.[8]

An interesting paradox can occur as we learn something new. Simply by heightening awareness of what is going on right now, we begin to improve. The act of self-reflection without judgment allows our bodies to find the right way to swing the racket and the right way to pay attention to another person.[9] (Relaxed concentration can be especially helpful as a tool to notice your own knee-jerk reactions as well as the ways in which others are responding to you.)

The Loose Moose Theatre in Calgary coaches its improvisers not to be prepared. This forces them to listen and respond in the moment to whatever is occurring.

Here are some things to focus on as you develop the skill of paying attention. A word of caution though. Don't attempt to pay attention to all these things at the same time. Focusing on too many things will pull you away from the relationship with the other person as you try to remember all the things you're supposed to notice. You might want to pick just one for starters.

- **Leaning in and leaning away.** How are others responding to your idea? Are they leaning in or leaning away? Are they building on your idea or blocking it? Do they seem interested? Do you pick up signals that indicate movement toward or away from you or your idea?
- **Reactions.** You can pay attention to the other person's reactions, your own reactions, and the interplay

between you. One area to pay attention to is emotion. Many anthropologists believe that there are six basic emotions: happiness, sadness, anger, fear, disgust, and surprise. Some would say (not without some controversy) that the way we show these emotions facially is universal and cuts across culture and race.[10]

What's important for us, however, is increasing our capacity to pick up subtle (and not so subtle) signals that indicate shifts in emotion in ourselves and in the other person. When Level 2 or Level 3 issues are alive, sensitivity to the world of emotions can be a powerful resource as you listen "with a willingness to be changed" and to influence the other person.

- **Talking and listening.** Is there a balance of speaking and listening? Is one person doing most of the talking? If so, what impact is this having on the exchange? According to Neil Rackham's research, better salespeople ask a lot more questions and listen a lot more than their less-successful counterparts. He refers to traditional salespeople as "talking brochures."[11]

- **Silence versus activity.** Does your conversation resemble Phil Spector's early Wall of Sound rock recordings, which left no holes in the aural fabric? If so, what impact does this Wall of Sound have? It worked for rock artists, but it doesn't work so well in conversation. (Sometimes people keep talking for fear that even a moment's silence will destroy the momentum.)

- **Physical signals.** Notice the physical ways in which the two of you make contact. For example, how do you position your bodies in relation to each other? What movement takes place in your facial muscles? Do your eyes meet or not? Are you able to maintain comfortable eye contact? Are you staring or darting away? Even something as simple as a smile can be a key. It's hard to fake a smile. We use different muscles when we smile naturally in contrast to those times when we fake delight.[12]

- **Communication style.** Notice how both of you use language. Take humor, for example. Does it help you "lean in" or does it seem to cause you to "lean away"? Does your communication style resemble a highly competitive tennis match in which one person makes most of the serves and the other person runs frantically around the court trying to volley?

As you put the principle of paying attention into practice, I'd suggest that initially you do only one thing different when you engage someone else: Just notice how you are paying attention. Imagine you are watching a television show. I doubt that you would yell commands at your favorite character, "No, Buffy, don't go in that haunted house again. How could you do that? You should know better." Try to give yourself the same latitude you'd give Buffy.

INTERVIEW WITH ALAN ALDA, actor and director

Many have said that acting is listening. Actors are taught how to pay attention to their partners and their surroundings in scenes. Alan Alda is a respected actor and director, probably best known for his work as Hawkeye Pierce in the television series "M.A.S.H." He takes paying attention a step further. He believes that actors must listen with a willingness to be changed. When this occurs, the audience can sense a vibrancy and vitality because the story feels new. The characters truly seem moved by what's going on around them.

RM: How do you personally prepare yourself to listen with a willingness to be changed?

AA: Before a performance I talk with the other actors for a long time. I get used to hearing them, seeing them, making them laugh, and letting them make me laugh. (I can't act with a total stranger.) I get comfortable with them. And we all get used to listening to one another because you can't laugh with someone you're not listening to.

When we're onstage, I carry that with me. I look at the person who is actually in front of me. I don't answer what I think they ought to be saying, but what they actually are saying and how they say it. I don't ignore obvious clues in their tone and body language.

I let every shift in the way they talk to me alter the way I respond. It doesn't matter that my character knows clearly what he wants from them. I can only attempt to get what I want by taking into account the way they just spoke to me. And if it's all happening right, all this changes with every performance. We'll all say the same lines and stand in the same places, but the sound and rhythms of our dialogue will be different every night.

RM: How do you stay open to the possibility of being changed with all the distractions that can occur on stage?
AA: If you pay attention to why you're out there, it would have to be a pretty big distraction to throw you off the track.

I believe that in a play I'm only allowed on stage in order to try to get what I want. If I ignore the obstacles the other person is putting in my way, then I'll only *pretend* to try to get what I want. It's in this way that my performance is really found in the other person's performance. I can't act without acting on them, and I can't truly act on them unless I actually see and hear what they're doing. This is what makes a play dynamic and worth watching. Otherwise it's a series of boring, alternating monologues.

RM: How do you catch yourself not listening fully?
AA: This is kind of subtle. It has to do with wanting to eliminate acting from a performance, if at all possible. When I hear myself acting, I realize I'm not listening. I just calm down and pay attention. Acting is not about how I do things, or how I sound, or how I look ... it's about how I try to get what I want from the person who is actually in front of me. Everything else is pretending and not very interesting. It's surprising how the simplest things can be made phony when an actor is content to pretend. Picking up a glass of water or putting on a pair of eyeglasses can become a three-act play in itself. Acting is not posing. And listening is not waiting.

CHAPTER 8

Explore Deeply

The handwriting was on the wall, but we thought it was a forgery.
— Executive at Harley Davidson, referring to the old days
when the company's reputation was diminishing

Jennifer Lawton is CEO of NET Daemons Associates, Inc. She circulates her annual business plan to all fifty-eight employees for their feedback and support. She expects people to express their opinions at the annual corporate meeting: "Our employees are very vocal." If employees don't speak publicly, they see her privately after the meeting. One employee questioned her projected annual growth rate of 100 to 200 percent. Lawton talked with the staff and revised her ambitious projections: "His question caused me to think about how that growth feels from an engineer's perspective."[1]

How many people do you know who willingly subject their plans to critique — and then actually revise their thinking based on the feedback they receive? I can't think of many either.

WHY EXPLORE DIFFERENCES?

If we want people to get excited about our ideas, we often need to be willing to be influenced by their thinking. For starters, what do they need from you? Do they understand the issue? Are they reacting against your idea? Do they trust you? Once you know why others oppose (or love) you or your idea, you have options:

- You can search for a way to combine what they want with what you want. Or . . .
- You might rec)gnize that their resistance actually makes sense. They have given you valuable information that causes you to rethink your idea. Or . . .
- You may find out that you are not likely to get agreement and that to proceed would be too risky or costly. Or . . .
- You may not agree with their objections, so you decide to proceed without their support.

Any of these options can be appropriate in the right circumstances. However, if your goal is to meet your objectives while maintaining a good working relationship, the last option can be a dangerous choice. Proceeding without the support of others often erodes or just outright demolishes relationships. If that seems like the only viable option, then it is best to do it with your eyes open. Proceed fully aware of the potential consequences — good and bad — of this choice.

Actually inviting disagreement may seem unnecessary and a waste of time. It isn't. If resistance is deep — Level 2 reaction against the idea or Level 3 mistrust — you must find out what's blocking agreement before you can hope to win their support.

If it is unusual to hear an engineer raise what could be a simple Level 1 question about projected growth rates in the company, think how rare it is to hear people give voice to their fears (Level 2 or Level 3). And the deeper levels are the ones that most often seriously block agreement. (Of course, what is a Level 1 concern today about projections could go to Level 2 once the engineers realize the toll they will pay for trying to meet this unreasonable target.)

If we are going for agreement, we must have reliable ways to get at good information — and that can be challenging.

WHAT MAKES EXPLORATION SO DIFFICULT?

I believe most people would prefer to speak openly and honestly with one another, but it seldom happens. It is more typical that people are reluctant or even afraid to tell the truth as they see it. If we want others to tell us why they oppose us or our idea, we have to make it safe for them to speak.

While there are many things that can inhibit candid conversation, three issues stand out.

The Need for Speed

Our desire to get a product to market, to make a sale, or to just get on with things may not allow room for the other person to speak. The message we send is: "Keep your criticism short, I'm busy, and I have more important things to do."

When people believe that you really don't have time for them, they may have a knee-jerk reaction. They might move against you by saying things in a strongly worded fashion. They might move away by simply not disclosing much. (When speed is the issue, it is less common to see people move toward you.)

A Belief That We Could Hurt Them

Never underestimate your ability to frighten people. It makes no difference that the fear of reprisal is only imagined. Imagination is the truth until you give people some reason to believe otherwise.

If your idea prompts a Level 2 emotional reaction, the person is afraid of something. Your idea threatens something in his life: job, power, status, control, self-respect, the respect of others. If you prompt Level 3 mistrust, then you (or your group) are causing the person to protect himself from you. As brain research shows, the fear response may be unconscious. If so, the person may not even know what he's not telling you because he doesn't know.[2]

Safety allows people to let down their guard, and when this occurs they may be able to be more reflective and begin to discover the real reasons why they oppose you or your idea.

Our Own Defensiveness

Even though you ask for an honest critique, you may be so wedded to your own idea (or your reputation) that you counter every comment with a rebuttal. When you should be listening attentively and asking questions that show your interest and willingness to explore, you stop every hint of exploration with a fusillade of words.

Some people join the battle and move against you with bullets of their own. Others move away, and some others move toward by showing interest in the poor pathetic person who is ranting and raving and they seek to accommodate you. In this instance, people may feel pity for you and give you a false agreement. It is only later that they realize they said yes, when deeper issues block their ability to make a real commitment to you or the idea.

In none of these instances does the other person give you much information about the real reasons why he or she opposes you.

Fear of the Unknown

In this instance, the unknown is usually emotional. Like seafarers reading ancient maps that warned, "Beyond here be dragons," we are reluctant to go into these uncharted waters. Instead of setting sail, we back off and blame emotions themselves as the culprit: "Oh, he's just too touchy-feely" or "She's too high maintenance."

We may be reluctant to follow television character Ally McBeal's advice to "free fall with the truth and hope we both survive."[3] And yet, it is this willingness to explore what we don't already know that can provide valuable information — the kind of information that may allow us find common interests, concerns, and aspirations.

WHAT IT TAKES TO EXPLORE EFFECTIVELY

Exploring differences is an unusual and untried strategy for most of us. This type of conversation takes us from the relative safety of I/It into a domain where I become keenly interested in You — your thoughts, your feelings, and your ideas and plans. When I shift from I/It, I give up certainty in favor of the unknown. Criticism can be painfully difficult to hear. In these instances, it is hard to keep listening openly. After all, someone is attacking us or our cherished idea. That can be hard to take. There are a few actions that I believe are necessary for deeper exploration:

- Shut up and listen
- Put your goal aside temporarily

- Be willing to be influenced by what you hear
- Go deeper than you'd probably like
- Be willing to seek common ground

Shut Up and Listen

When we have an idea, we may listen just long enough to hear a major objective and then go on the offensive: "Thanks for sharing your views, but now let me tell you why you're wrong." When this occurs, the other person is likely to parry the blow, and little new information comes into the conversation. We both are trying to win.

Someone once said, "During your lifetime you'll be given many opportunities to shut up. Take advantage of all of them."

Put Your Goal Aside Temporarily

As we listen to someone else criticize our plan or ourselves, we may begin to believe that listening equals surrender. When this belief kicks in, we are likely to redouble our efforts to sell our idea or give up — fight or flight.

One of the seven habits of highly effective people identified by Stephen Covey is "seek first to understand." He writes, "If I were to summarize the single most important principle I have learned in interpersonal communications, it would be this: *seek first to understand, and then be understood.* This principle is key to effective interpersonal communication."[4] Covey is not suggesting that we abandon our dreams, but that we be willing to see the world from the other person's perspective and then decide what to do next.

COFFEE WITH JOE

Every office has a Joe. This person will tell you the truth as he or she sees it. Joe has no sense of office politics and will just tell you what he or she thinks. As hard as it may be to talk with this person, Joe might be able to help you prepare for an exchange with someone else. I recall a client in a federal agency who had a Joe on his staff. Joe was a whiner and seemed to be unhappy much of the time. But he said things no one else dared say to the boss. I urged my client to listen to Joe and ask himself, "What are the implications if Joe is speaking for others on this issue?"

When U.S. Ambassador Averell Harriman first met Soviet Premier Nikita Khrushchev, he allowed him to rant and rave at Americans for two days. After Khrushchev got that out, they were able to talk.[5] Had Harriman protested, counterpunched, walked out, or shown an unwillingness to take the heat, it is unlikely they could have reached a point where they could talk with one another.

Be Willing to Be Influenced by What You Hear

If our minds are already made up, we shouldn't ask what the other person thinks. It's insulting, and when people realize what we're doing, their resistance is likely to increase.

Listening with a willingness to be influenced suggests that we are open to hearing things that are new and different. In his book *On Dialogue*, Robert Grudin writes that reciprocity and strangeness are the keys to successful dialogue: "By reciprocity I mean a give-and-take between two or more minds. . . . This give-and-take is open-ended and is not controlled or limited by any single participant. By strangeness I mean the shock of new information — divergent opinion, unpredictable data, sudden emotion, etc. — on those to whom it is expressed. Reciprocity and strangeness carry dialogue far beyond a mere conversation between two monolithic information sources. Through reciprocity and strangeness, dialogue becomes an evolutionary process in which the parties are changed as they proceed."[6]

Go Deeper Than You'd Probably Like

Exploring differences often triggers our knee-jerk reactions. When this occurs, we may want to cut things short. Our brains may tell us, "I've heard enough." We might even delude ourselves into thinking that we understand the person's concerns and now it's time to move on. We believe we aren't really giving in to a knee-jerk reaction. We truly believe we have taken in what they had to say and now it is time to move forward. We'd be wrong.

It is hard to have people question us at all three levels. Imagine that they don't agree with our thinking, they think our idea will harm them, and they think we're the wrong person for the job. In those instances, we may begin to feel our knee quivering, and yet, the best game in town is to keep exploring.

DEVELOP WORST-CASE SCENARIOS

If you're nervous about traveling with Dante, you could create a worst-case scenario to help you plan some ways to explore for information, emotional reactions, and things that might inhibit trust. There are two reasons why this makes sense.

- **The scenario puts your own fears out in the open.** Sometimes fear far outweighs the actual risk. Imagining what might happen can be a helpful reality check.
- **It allows you to plan.** If you decide to proceed, you can prepare an overall strategy for staying engaged. The scenario will help you identify those places that might cause a knee-jerk reaction. Then you can determine how to support yourself during the exchange and what you can do to regain your balance if you do begin to lose control of your actions.

In my experience, people usually don't go deep enough. It's like Dante making it to the Third Circle of Hell, looking around, and saying to himself, "Well that's about far enough for today. This looks like paradise to me."

When we stop short of fully exploring, we run the risk of cutting off the possibility of I/You contact. Remember, Covey isn't suggesting that we seek first to understand just a little bit. If we're going to explore, we have to make a commitment to the entire journey. During Dante's journey, he wanted to turn back many times, but faith allowed him to keep going through nine Circles of Hell and another nine Circles of Purgatory, knowing that paradise would be at the other end.

OK, perhaps calling the destination paradise may be a bit of a stretch. However, I've seen people who have had the guts to stick with exploration through all the circles create dramatic shifts in their relationships, which led to both sides seeing possibilities that neither thought possible before the journey.

We have to listen until we bleed. In other words, keep exploring to find out the real issues that concern the other person. The temptation can be to keep the exploration limited to Level 1 issues, such as cost estimates, timing, and such. That would be like Dante trying to find paradise simply by wandering around somewhere near the gates of Hell but never taking the risk to enter through gates that read, "Abandon all hope, ye who enter here."[7]

Another way of going deeper is to accept blame. During the Northern Ireland peace process, the chairmen took blame for the delays in the talks, even though it was not their fault.[8] And of course, taking responsibility for a mistake when it truly is ours can go a long way to increase people's confidence in us.

Self-deprecating humor can help as well. My friend Jeanette is a comic in London. Most comics are in their twenties, as are their audiences. She is older. She often opens her show with, "Good evening. I know what you're all thinking, 'What's me mum doing here tonight?' Those who are happy to see me, you've got a good relationship with your mum. The rest of you, go home and work it out." People laugh and she has them on her side. Many often try to keep hidden what the rest of the world already knows. Jeanette just says it. Humor directed toward ourselves can be a powerful ally.

Be Willing to Seek Common Ground

The work of The Common Ground Network for Life and Choice shows that some version of paradise is possible if we stick with these principles. The Network was established to facilitate dialogue between pro-life and pro-choice advocates who wanted to search for common ground on the abortion question. They created a process that allowed people to speak, listen, and be influenced by one another. What surprised many people who took part was just how much common ground there was between the two groups. For example, both sides often showed deep concern for the welfare of women and children in our country, the epidemic use of drugs by children, and the high number of unwanted teen pregnancies. These conversations allowed people to see past their Level 3 positions and begin to see human beings who had hopes and fears just like they did.[9]

If you listen deeply and fully, paying attention to what's different, surprising, even strange — and listen to where your ideas may be similar or build on one another's — you have a chance to find a mutually agreeable solution.

THE CHALLENGE AND THE HOPE

Is applying these actions difficult? Yes. In some situations (especially Level 3), it can take all the energy you have to pay attention and avoid knee-jerk reactions.

Martin is a middle manager and has an idea for a new way that his department could achieve better customer service. He believes that customers should be brought into the planning process. This is not a novel concept in many organizations, but it would be a radical departure for his group. While the department head and others have a pretty open policy about hearing ideas from anyone, Martin has gained a reputation as a naysayer. His ideas tend to poke holes in the existing order of things. People find him tiring and tend to tune out or argue with him when he presents his ideas for improvement.

Fortunately, he realized that his way of presenting his ideas was probably going to be his undoing. So he tried a different approach. He presented his idea clearly and simply, and then he tried to follow the actions covered in this section. He promised himself that once he explained his idea he would shut up and listen. And he would allow himself to be influenced by what he heard.

He was amazed, but his own thinking shifted as a result of what he heard. By the end of the meeting, they had come up with a plan that looked a bit different from Martin's original idea, but it was still a very good way to address the customer service challenge.

MORE WAYS TO EXPLORE DEEPLY

There are some additional things that can help you explore and not elicit or revert to knee-jerk reactions.

Find a Safe Way to Talk

Negotiators know that talks need to take place on neutral ground. Where you engage people can make a significant difference in how the talks go. There are many ways to create a safe space, though there is no one-size-fits-all structure that supports exploration. Using I/You as a guide, you might ask yourself, "What will work best for both of us?" Perhaps it is a conference room or a restaurant. And even e-mail can work!

In a guest op-ed piece for *USA Today*, Anne Glauber described her interaction with her teenaged daughter over what constituted appropriate dress for school: "Every morning followed the same routine, a hostile clash of two women's wills, jostling for power. . . . It wore us down, minute by minute, argument by argument. Yet neither of us would admit defeat. In fact, despite our battle weariness, our antagonism escalated. Both of us discarded rational arguments for the satisfying but short-lived victories of nasty digs."[10] Sound familiar?

Glauber had always dismissed e-mail as a medium that would not allow "real conversations and deep encounters," but one morning, out of frustration, she sent her daughter an e-mail. "I wrote her logically and calmly about my sadness that we were increasingly unable to communicate," she said. And she included how much she loved her daughter. Later in the day, her daughter responded through e-mail. She stated her position logically and why dressing in the way she did was important to her.

"Through our daily e-mails we not only reached a compromise on the clothes . . . but we also cut through to other issues and reinforced how much we respected and loved each other."

Listen to Grok

In *Stranger in a Strange Land*, author Robert Heinlein invented the word "grok" to describe a condition where one character (it was science fiction, so not all characters were people) fully grasps what the other is about.[11] To grok is far more than just reaching an intellectual understanding; it is like grasping the situation in our bones. We grok the content of the message and why it is important to the other person. We understand the assumptions behind their beliefs. We take in their values. Their fears. Why they say what they say. That's hard to do. (Maybe that's why it's science fiction.)

Exploring differences is enhanced when we are willing to attempt to grok the world from another's point of view and then, as Alan Alda suggests, listen with a willingness to be changed. This is a powerful combination that can allow us to find common ground where none seemed to exist before.

This type of deep listening has a little to do with skills and a lot to do with intent. If I keep the I/You spirit in mind as I listen with a strong desire to fully understand and a willingness to be influenced, the skills often take care of themselves.

Put Skin in the Game

Up to now, it could appear that all we need to do during this phase of the conversation is listen. Throw in a few "hmmms," and an occasional "I see what you mean," and that's all there is to it. But we need to do much more.

We need to show that we are in the game as well. We need to be willing to show our own excitement. We need to be willing to express our concern or fear when appropriate. (After all, that is exactly what we are asking from the other person.)

We need to listen in ways that invite exploration from both of us. When she says something that shifts your thinking, let her know. When she says something that you think might make a great alternative to your suggestion, acknowledge it. When what she says frightens you, consider being candid about your emotions as well.

This is not to suggest that you do all the work. Expressing your own deep-seated vulnerability when the other person is not revealing anything may be too risky. In ballroom dancing, partners support each other. One partner can only lean back as far as the other's physical support allows.

Understand — It may be tempting to stick with Level 1 informational considerations as you explore. That could be a big mistake. Usually, the real data lies in the reactions and trust levels.

React — If they react against your idea it probably stems from fear. From their vantage point, there is something dangerous about your idea. You explore to find out more about Level 2 concerns.

Trust — It is often very difficult for people to tell us the truth regarding the trust or distrust they have in us. Exploration sometimes needs to be slow and cautious.

When dancing with a new partner, each gauges how adventurous to be based on the signals received from the other. Weaker dancers will wait for their partner to test conditions. Better dancers keep testing the limits of this support in minute ways to see how far they can go. You can see good dancers who are out on the floor together for the first time begin with easy moves, and by the end of the dance they make an observer gasp with delight.

Put Limits on the Work

Just as the walls of an oven keep a fire contained, putting clear boundaries around a conversation allows us to use the heat constructively. Without those walls, a fire can rage out of control. The same can happen in intense discussions.

Keeping our initial intent in mind can be very helpful. Like an actor's overall objective for his character or Dante's vision of paradise, we know the direction we want to travel. Say my overall intent is to have some version of my idea accepted in a way that works for you. When I explore our differences, I will limit my exploration to issues that affect acceptance of my idea. Perhaps there may be many other issues that I believe we should talk about, but it's better to save those for another time. If this encounter works well, we might explore other issues later. This occurred when Anne Glauber engaged her daughter over the issue of dress. As the relationship built over time, they were able to begin to explore other things. But they started small.

Think about what is possible and doable given your relationship and the amount of time you have. Limiting the work to what may be possible can allow both of you to relax. We enter the conversation knowing that at least for today there won't be a blood bath.

Respect the Other Person's Distance

Limiting the work also includes showing respect for another's reluctance to speak with you. Just because you want to talk and explore the deeper issues doesn't mean that the other person does. If your relationship has been based on a Level 3 historic animosity, he may not want to come over and play with you today.

It is important to create a structure that allows exploration in a way that is comfortable for both of you. In these ultra-intense situations, you may not get much, but using I/You as a guide, you will probably find that today's conversation is a small step in a direction that you'd like to see.

When conditions make conversation difficult, it may be a mistake to push for open conversation. Conditions may require that you rebuild bridges that have been destroyed. And that takes time. Chapter 11 covers ideas for building stronger working relationships.

KNOWING WHEN YOU'VE EXPLORED ENOUGH

An amazing thing can happen when we explore differences effectively: Sometimes that is all the work that needs to be done. Things just seem to work out. The fact that we are really listening may make it easier for someone to listen to us. Trust begins to build. As we dig deep, with a willingness to be influenced, we both begin to take more interest in what the other

If we listen with a willingness to be changed, we make it easier for the other person to join us in that exploration. How do we know when we've explored this issue sufficiently? Here are some things to listen for:

- When you test the waters and people seem eager to discuss ways of proceeding
- When the other person begins to suggest ways of moving ahead
- When pronouns shift from you to us
- When you feel less guarded and can feel yourself speaking more candidly and with greater ease
- When it feels like a weight has just lifted
- When the skies open, harps play, and choirs sing (Just kidding, I'm still waiting for that one.)

is saying. Both of us may begin to see common interests, hopes, wishes, and fears. Possibilities emerge.

Salespeople are always looking for ways to test the waters to know when the customer is ready to make a decision. Neil Rackham's advice is quite simple: Just ask, "Have I answered all your questions? Is there anything else I can provide for you?"[12]

Often the ability to pay attention is a critical skill in knowing when you've explored enough. And once we have explored issues sufficiently, it is time to see if it is possible to connect their wishes with ours.

INTERVIEW WITH LYNNE JACOBS, therapist and psychoanalyst

Lynne Jacobs and Gary Yontef, founders of the Gestalt Therapy Institute of the Pacific (Los Angeles), developed an approach to therapy that they refer to as relational. I've seen them give demonstrations and the results are amazing. Like a good friend, they just get very interested in the client's story. They seem keenly interested in how this person sees things — and they do this without a hint of judgment or admonishment. They explore what gets evoked in the exchange that's occurring between them right there in the office. Often, this exchange is the work that needs to be done. On the surface this may seem simple, but the impact on the client (and on them) is often profound. Through a willingness to engage their clients with the intention of supporting I/You, healing takes place.

RM: How is a relational approach different from more traditional ways of working?
LJ: Everything that happens in the therapy office is shared. The patient's behavior and experience are co-created with the therapist. Nothing that the patient does arises merely from the patient. So those who work from a relational stance try to focus their attention on the impact on the patient of what's occurring between them, because that's what's vivid right then.

RM: What does that look like?

LJ: It's the difference between looking at the patient and making assessments from the outside versus trying to look at the same movie the patient is looking at. Trying to get as close as possible to seeing what the patient's life experiences must be like.

RM: Not to judge, but to understand?

LJ: Yes.

RM: You're bright, you've got a lot of experience, and you're an expert in your field. Why not just tell clients what they should do?

LJ: One of the things I've noticed is that patients have invested a tremendous amount of hope in the therapeutic relationship and with that comes a tremendous amount of dread as well. They tend to react with their defenses when their hopes are disappointed — and their hopes have to get disappointed. If I stand outside and assess the patients, they may feel like objects. That brings up shame, defensiveness, and annoyance — stuff like that. Those reactions don't tend to be very useful in the early stages when they are endeavoring to be understood. So it's important for me to establish more accepting contact with them.

RM: How do you do that?

LJ: I ask myself, "What's it like to be in their shoes right now?" Obviously, I'm not going to have the same emotional reactions if I'm seeing things from their side.

RM: I would think they would find this very supportive and make it easier for them to do their work.

LJ: I think people come to therapy because they've been wounded in their efforts to relate intimately to others, and they've built up defenses to protect themselves from injuries. The therapeutic relationship helps them recapture resilience in the face of difficult emotions. It is through our emotions that we feel alive. I think the relationship in therapy is probably one of the most important, if not the most important, supports for helping someone learn to recognize their moment-to-moment experience.

RM: It sounds like the relational approach allows patients to experience emotions with another person in a relatively safe environment, and that begins to build their capacity to handle emotions in their lives.

LJ: Yes. When I first started using this approach many years ago, my patients felt more able to tell me — or live through with me — more vulnerable dimensions of their existence than they had been able to before. All of the patients who were with me then commented on the shift.

RM: What do you do during those times when it is challenging to stay that open to the other person?

LJ: When I'm feeling troubled, it is usually because I'm feeling at the mercy of the patient. So the best way for me to break out of that loop where I am just reactive and annoyed, angry, or defensive is to try to see things from their side. I simply need to remind myself that it always makes me feel better to do that.

RM: A final question: When you adopted the relational approach, did you notice any changes in yourself outside of work?

LJ: Once I got into the habit of listening from an empathetic perspective — which means getting what it's like to be in the other person's shoes — it made me more open-hearted. I'm more likely to have a kind of sympathetic take on why somebody might be doing the things they are doing, even if it's bothersome to me. I feel like I walk through the world with more grace and more love.

CHAPTER 9

Find Ways to Connect

It is the mark of a good action that its appeal is inevitable in retrospect.
— Adlai Stevenson, American politician (1900–1965)

Exploration is in service of connection. The most reliable way to build support for our ideas occurs when we blend our intentions with the other person's. And it is the only game in town if we need support and commitment. You can't force commitment; at best, you may get compliance to the letter of the law if someone is afraid to oppose you openly.

There are other reasons to seek mutual wins as well. You now have two heads thinking, getting excited, and worrying about this issue. When your issue is my issue, I do more than just keep my promises: I look for ways to make this idea a success.

And reaching mutual agreement is like money in the bank. When people see you seriously want to work with them, they are far more likely to give you the benefit of any doubts when you come up with your next suggestion.

Imagine the weekly meeting between a chief financial officer (CFO) and a chief medical officer (CMO) regarding the budget of a hospital:

> CFO: What's this line item about a renal scanning device?
> CMO: (with pride) It's a new, highly regarded diagnostic
>   tool that picks up kidney problems in ways that —
> CFO: (interrupting) Is this price a misprint?
> CMO: Well you know, state-of-the-art equipment isn't cheap.
> CFO: I guess not! Chris, we don't do all that much kidney
>   work here.

CMO: But those we do treat deserve the best we can offer. You have to agree with that.

CFO: True, but our patient outcome stats are fine these days. A new machine might be nice, but we can't afford one.

CMO: (sighs and looks at others with a "Can you believe what I've got to put up with?" look)

And on it goes. The only thing that changes from meeting to meeting is the item in question. This week it's a renal scanning device, next time it will be something else. Just listening to the words, it may appear that this is a Level 1 exchange based on information. They are arguing over the questions: "Can we afford it?" and "Do we need it?"

But the issue is deeper than Level 1 for both the CMO and the CFO — although neither seems to know it. The CFO might think: "All the CMO cares about is getting the most elaborate equipment with no appreciation of the costs involved. We could go out of business, that wouldn't bother Chris, as long as we had the new equipment."

The CMO might say: "All the CFO cares about is money. How to cut costs. Every time you look, Pat's finding some way to make it harder for us to do our jobs."

Both would be wrong.

If they had explored more deeply instead of fencing with each other, the CMO would have learned that the CFO cares deeply about patient care, but believes it is the CFO's job to ensure that the hospital is operating in a fiscally responsible manner. The CFO would have learned that the CMO cared deeply about providing good patient care. This is the reason why the CMO chose the medical profession. But the CFO would have been surprised to learn that the CMO understood that a healthcare institution couldn't just throw money around, that fiscal responsibility made sense.

A PROCESS FOR CONNECTING

Exploring allows us to get at the reasons behind the reasons. Connecting allows us to turn that deep resistance into support. Knowing the reasons behind the resistance allows us to reframe the conversation into one that embraces both sides of the issue.

Imagine that Pat (the CFO) wanted to find a way to connect with Chris. Here is a process that can help.

1. **Identify the real fear or concern.** Pat and Chris's arguments don't get at the real concerns. They need to explore their differences more deeply. Pat might take time at the next meeting to listen and test her assumptions. Her goal will be to find out what's really important for the CMO. Throughout the conversation, Pat will check her assumptions to make sure she is taking in what Chris has to say.
2. **State what's most important to you.** In Pat's case, it is fiscal responsibility. She wants to make sure the hospital continues to have sufficient reserves so they can pay their bills, even if they have a few bad months.
3. **Turn that statement of concern into a statement of what you both want.** Once Pat thinks she has delved to the root of the issue for Chris and stated what she wants, she might ask, "Would you be willing to work with me on finding a way to provide great quality care while ensuring that we keep costs in line?"

If Chris is interested in exploring that question, they can begin to work on ways to meet this dual objective.

EMBRACE THE PARADOX

Grappling with two opposing points at the same time is challenging. It may even seem paradoxical to try to reconcile these opposing forces. How in the world could you ever provide high quality care and keep costs low? And yet, it's the very tension between these two poles that allows us to find mutual wins.

It's rare to find people sticking with disagreements long enough to find common ground. Consequently, opportunities to influence — and be influenced in return — turn into win-lose battles. We fight for low costs. The other person fights for quality care. Someone will win, someone will lose. Creating a paradoxical question allows you to see whether a mutual win is possible. Here are examples of statements some of my clients created that embrace fundamental paradoxes in their work:

- How can we cut costs and still fund all other projects?
- How can we commit resources to this new project while meeting other critical objectives?
- How can we reduce customer requirements while maintaining great customer relations?
- How can we economically implement enterprise resource management and meet current budget targets at the same time?
- How can we implement a new promotion policy while guaranteeing that we still reward the best performers?
- How can we centralize major human resources tracking information while maintaining significant local control of HR in the regions?

A Template

As you've no doubt picked up, the template for one of these questions is quite simple: "How can we do A while ensuring B?" But in order for that simple question to achieve a mutual win, it must contain the following:

- **The B portion must be a core issue for the other party.** You must make it easy for the person to say, "That's important."
- **The B portion needs to be stated positively.** Instead of saying "without cutting jobs," it is stronger to say "while ensuring full employment." You are not just avoiding a negative (losing jobs) but moving toward a positive (ensuring employment).
- **The tension between A and B needs to be strong and exciting.** It should make the other person think, "Is that really possible?" in a way that makes it inviting to join you in conversation. The statement acts like a magnet, attracting people to engage in a conversation with you.

Rhino Foods is a sixty-person producer of ingredients for dessert products. In the early 1990s, founder and president Ted Castle announced that the company had to cut costs dramatically. Because wages and benefits were the largest line item, he saw downsizing as the only choice. He didn't want to cut people and was open to hearing other suggestions. The employees at Rhino came up with 111 alternatives to downsizing! A committee bundled similar suggestions and selected the ones that would give the most benefit. Rhino was able to weather the bad economic times without a single layoff.

In effect, Castle invited people to join him in addressing this dilemma: "How can we cut costs significantly while ensuring full employment?" There is no guarantee that just by asking the question there will be a way to cut costs without layoffs — but there is no way of achieving that goal if it is never even considered.

Pre-existing Conditions

The paradoxical question alone is not enough. A few conditions must be in place for it to work. Ted Castle's approach met both of these conditions:

- **Room to join you.** This can't be a done deal. If so, there is no need for the conversation. In fact, holding a conversation when your mind is already made up is simply manipulation, and you'll deserve the resistance you'll get when people figure that out.
- **Willingness to be influenced.** The goals themselves can be strong (we need to cut costs by 20 percent), but you still need to be open in how you'll achieve them. For example, the CEO and board of a small company decided to merge with another company. That decision was a done deal, but the CEO was open to exploring with staff from both facilities ways to make the merger work successfully for them.

Ted Castle said this about the approach they used at Rhino Foods: "Not only did we avoid the stress and pain that laid-off employees and their families feel, we built a level of trust at the company that's impossible to measure."[1] In 1997, Rhino did have to lay off some workers. However, Castle was able to use the approaches his team identified in the early '90s three times over the years before they had to resort to actual downsizing.[2]

In *Polarity Management*, Barry Johnson suggests that paradoxes such as cost versus employment security are a part of life. He believes these paradoxes can't be solved, but need to be managed or else we run the risk of swinging back and forth from one pole to the other repeatedly.[3] (I highly recommend his book as a way to learn more about working with polarities.)

OTHER WAYS TO CONNECT

Creating a statement that embraces both sides of the issue is one way to try to connect, but there are others. Here are three that I think are particularly useful.

The Believing Game

When Peter Elbow taught college writing, he found that students had difficulty listening to each other's critiques. They tended to tear down without seeking to understand first. He began to realize that good thinking involves skepticism and critique and an ability to appreciate as well. Elbow writes, "Yes, we need the systematic, disciplined, and conscious attempt to criticize everything no matter how compelling it might seem — to find flaws or contradictions we might otherwise miss. But thinking is not trustworthy unless it also includes methodological belief: the equally systematic, disciplined, and conscious attempt to believe everything no matter how unlikely or repellant it might seem — to find virtues or strengths we might otherwise miss."[4] He calls these two approaches the Doubting Game and the Believing Game.

Most of us are quite adept at the Doubting Game. The history of philosophy has instilled the Doubting Game in us. Much of our educational system is based on this game. Teachers search for what is wrong, believing that finding errors will help a student improve. Many who attend corporate meetings use this game to punch holes in proposals. It can be a very effective tool, but it is limited.

The Believing Game is a complement to this approach. The "critic" attempts to look at the world through the eyes of the other person and offer his or her opinion as a way of helping this person build on the idea. So rather than tearing down, it builds on what is offered. It is not soft. The critique can be incisive as the manager or teacher or critic seeks clarity and sound reasons to help the person make his or her case.

I am not suggesting that you give up the Doubting Game, but that you also include the Believing Game in your repertoire. John Kander and Fred Ebb, the writers of such Broadway and film musicals as *Chicago*, *Funny Lady*, *Kiss of the Spider Woman*, and *New York, New York*, have their own version of this game. If one of them is excited about an idea, the other goes along just to see where it will go. When one became interested in Christopher

Isherwood's *Berlin Stories* as the foundation for a new musical, the other was skeptical. How could a collection of stories about the last days of the Weimar Republic be appropriate for a musical? One of the partners played his own version of the Believing Game and followed the passion of his partner, exploring "What if?" questions about turning the stories into a play. The result was the award-winning *Cabaret*.

A Trial Balloon Proposal

Imagine that Betty wanted to contract with Craig's Web design firm to develop a new e-business site for her company. She could not afford to pay his fees up-front. She knew he had cash-flow challenges and

Understand — Seeking a connection increases the understanding of both parties. You are exploring possibilities of what could be together.

React — With both of you leaning in to find a solution, you greatly increase the chance of gaining a favorable reaction.

Trust — If this principle is used after exploring and finding out what's really important, you give yourself the greatest opportunity to build trust.

probably would not accept deferred payment. (Money was a survival issue for Craig's company.) She presented a proposal for ways they might work together that deferred part of the payment and in exchange gave his firm a percentage of Web-based sales over the first six months. She offered the proposal as a trial balloon to give him something to respond to. The proposal was not a take-it-or-leave-it document. It was a working paper that he could accept, adapt, or use as the basis for a counteroffer.

Here's why this approach can work:

- **Turns concerns into positives.** Betty built her proposal on her knowledge of Craig's likely reaction, given his Level 2 survival issues. She would get nowhere if she ignored his cash flow concerns. If he accepted the proposal, his company could stand to make more money.
- **Seeks mutual wins.** Betty's proposal attempted to find a way for both companies to win from this venture.
- **Open to influence.** Even though Betty had given her proposal a lot of thought, she was willing to let it go. It was only a trial balloon. Her underlying stance was that she cared about finding something both could agree to.

Win-Win Lite

Not every situation requires a deep exploration of differences. When Guy Kawasaki still developed software products, he needed to get the support of reviewers. He says, "Often, journalists and reviewers gave me feedback about how to change a piece of software, and assuming I could convince the programmers, I tried to accommodate their suggestions. Were the reviewers' ideas significant improvements? Not really. Would it take a lot to change the software? Not really. But making the change flattered them and reduced the likelihood that they would pan a product that they had 'designed.'"[5] While I'm not wild about the condescending tone I read in his comments, his approach did allow him to be influenced to some degree by others.

In a similar fashion, Hollywood scriptwriters Jason Ward and David Garrett pitch story ideas to studios in a way that invites support. They present the concept of the movie in one sentence, "For *Corky*, this is a reverse *Donnie Brasco*." It is presented in a shorthand language the studio people understand. People in that business would immediately connect with the reference to the film *Donnie Brasco*. "The more they like it," Ward says, "the fewer specific details you should give. You want to let them fill in the blanks themselves for whatever kind of movie they would like to see."[6]

CONTINUOUS CONNECTION

These principles support ways to create stronger ties with others, so that each idea doesn't begin another long uphill struggle. They can help us increase understanding, build favorable reactions to our suggestions, and build trust.

Using the six principles of engagement — know your intention, consider the context, avoid knee-jerk reactions, pay attention, explore deeply, and find a way to connect — is a discipline, not a checklist of six easy steps. These principles are the foundation that influences what we say and do. They offer us a way to get back on track when we're at risk of derailing. They allow us to debrief situations that don't go so well and to begin to see where we need to pay closer attention and where we may need to change our behavior.

Part III explores ways to stay calm enough so you can actually apply these principles, as well as ways to shift the Level 3 conditions in favor of the relationship before you get into serious conflict with others. The final chapter is a discussion of when engaging may be the wrong option and you might consider waiting awhile or leaving.

INTERVIEW WITH NEIL RACKHAM, researcher and author on effective sales

Neil Rackham researches the practices of salespeople. In his books *SPIN Selling* (McGraw-Hill) and *Major Account Sales Strategy* (McGraw-Hill), he debunks the common wisdom of sales training that's been around since the 1920s. He found that what works if you're trying to sell a small item such as a toaster simply doesn't work if you are trying to influence people to make a major decision. The value of his insight extends beyond the world of sales to any of us who need to influence others as part of our work.

RM: What's the difference between successful and unsuccessful salespeople?
NR: At its most basic, it's a question of focus. The successful salesperson is focused on the customer and the needs of that customer. The less successful salesperson is focused on the product or service they are selling.

RM: What does that look like?
NR: The less successful salesperson tends to be a talking brochure. It is a very inefficient and expensive way of communicating a product and what it does. Successful salespeople work through questions. They ask questions that get the customers to think about their needs and their problems. They ask questions in a helpful sort of way that results in a greater understanding by the customer of the key issues.

RM: Your research suggests that there are very different types of questions a salesperson might ask. Some helpful, some not.
NR: It's worthwhile asking, Who does the question help? Who benefits from the question? If I ask you a lot of questions about your company, about your position, about the kind of products you're

INTERVIEW WITH NEIL RACKHAM (continued)

using at the moment, it doesn't do anything for you. All it does is tell me about how I'm going to sell to you. Those kinds of questions — called situation questions — exist for the benefit of the salesperson, not for the benefit of the customer. Not only don't they add any value to the customer's experience with you, they take up the customer's time. They have a negative value.

We find there are more of those kinds of questions in sales that fail. For a sale to succeed, salespeople must ask questions that matter to the customer. They're focusing on asking questions that probe down under the surface and really examine the problem in depth. We call those implication questions.

RM: Is this true across cultures?
NR: The value of questions that probe implications has been validated by research studies in thirty-five countries. And in every one of those thirty-five countries, successful salespeople were asking more implication questions than the less successful salespeople.

RM: Your research stands traditional sales methods on their head. Conventional sales wisdom suggests that you should constantly check to see if a customer is ready to make a decision. You suggest that using these closing techniques actually works against making a sale on major items. Why is that?
NR: Most closing methods and techniques focus on applying pressure to get the customer to buy. When you try to close you're putting pressure on the customer to make a decision. There's a simple law in psychology: the bigger the decision, the more negative the effect of pressure. If I'm trying to persuade you to have another cup of coffee, it's probably easier for you to accept it rather than have a fight about it. But if I'm trying to persuade you to change something major about your life and I pressure you, all I'll do is create resistance and get a fight.

RM: How do you know if a customer is ready to make a decision?
NR: You ask them! "Have we covered all the things that you want to cover? Is there any other area that is on your mind where you'd like more information? Is there something else that we can do that would be helpful to you?" Let the customers tell you when they

are ready to move on. So many salespeople don't do that. They just don't check with the customer to see if there are other issues or concerns.

RM: This seems related to some of your early research on the differences between push and pull styles of influence. Would you say a little about the differences between push and pull?
NR: There are the people who influence by the push style. It is enthusiasm, energy, persuasive urging, overwhelming others with evidence and facts, and really having a tremendous conviction in what you are doing.

RM: Is the push style effective?
NR: It generally works if you've got power. If you are the boss and can really push your people — or you are the expert people admire because everyone thinks you know what you are talking about.

RM: What about the pull style?
NR: The pull style works by trying to pull things you want out of the other person. I may want you to cooperate with me in a project. So, rather than using the push style and saying why this is such a great project, I say, "What are your ideas about how this project might be approached? I'd like to hear your thoughts on how we might structure this." I get your basic thoughts and then I build on them. By doing that, you feel much more commitment because you feel it is your idea.

RM: In my experience, push is used a lot in organizations on major changes, when pull would be a lot more effective.
NR: Say we're implementing a major change and I try to push it. I can have vision, great enthusiasm, and come in and really try to make it happen. But the moment my back is turned, the change slips backward. Maybe I could make things happen but I would have to be present all the time.

In contrast, if I use the pull style and have drawn the basic ideas out of other people, they feel very committed to those ideas and they'll make them work even when I'm not there. You can't police major changes all the time. So, if you want people to take ownership and manage their own change, you have to do it through a pull style rather than a push style.

PART III

The Fine Points of Influence and Engagement

CHAPTER 10

Stay Calm to Stay Engaged

We do not make decisions, decisions make themselves,
but only if we've allowed ourselves to prepare the ground
by passionately exploring all the options.

— Peter Brook, theater director

You can't stay calm when you are off balance. Watch any of Akira Kurasawa's classic Samurai films to see this at play. The Samurai went into battle calmly. They were alert and could respond instantly to whatever was placed in front of them. The tension that comes from worry about an imagined attack would detract from their ability to stay focused. Even in the midst of flying objects, punches, thrusts, and swords swiping at them, they remained calm.

The martial artist's calm is an alert state of readiness. I asked Jason, a black belt in the Japanese martial art of Aikido, if all his practice over the years made a difference in his day-to-day life. "Absolutely," he said. "I handle conflict much differently. Something happens to the wiring in your brain when you spend a few evenings every week watching people run at you with the intent of hurting you."

There is no shortcut to developing mastery in a martial art or in learning ways to influence while keeping the focus on I and You. It takes hard work, a willingness to learn from experience, and an ability to remain poised, alert, and relaxed. And, in playwright Samuel Beckett's words, a willingness to fail, fail again, and fail better. This chapter examines ways to develop the skill of a calm but alert readiness. It focuses on the fine points of preparing for meeting the other person and also explores ways to support yourself during the exchange.

PREPARE TO MEET THE OTHER PERSON

A calm and alert re idiness comes from noticing what is happening without judgment. It is being open to whatever happens. Things could be going according to plan or they could be blowing up in your face, but this way of being allows you to notice what's going on without becoming overwhelmed. When we judge our actions — "I'm doing really well now" or "I'm really blowing it this time" — that evaluation takes us away from the other person. Our attention goes inward and we begin to lose the focus on I and You.

As I mentioned earlier, Timothy Gallwey suggests that students use relaxed concentration to simply see tennis strokes as they are. He doesn't want them to consciously change anything, just notice. This acute and relaxed attention is what allows us to change. The strokes "must be perceived clearly. This can only be done when personal judgment is absent. As soon as a stroke is seen clearly and accepted as it is, a natural and speedy process of change begins."[1]

Imagine you are a secretary. You have an idea that could improve efficiency in your work with your boss, but it will require her to alter how she hands out assignments. As you present your idea, you notice that you are tightly clutching the folder you are holding and your grip just seems to relax. You notice her expression as you present your idea. It looks as though she is listening in a condescending manner. As you start to get angry, you simply note that you are getting angry. The anger subsides some. You realize that you are doing almost all the talking. Your boss couldn't respond if she wanted to. This realization causes you to smile at yourself, finish your sentence, and give her time to react. As she speaks, you note that you aren't paying attention to her; you're thinking about your rebuttal. Without even trying, this awareness allows you to refocus on what she is saying.

The skill you, as the secretary, were beginning to apply is no different from the one the tennis player, the martial artist, or the musician might use to stay focused. It is based on a willingness to be mindful of what is going on without judging everything as it comes up. The key to learning to be mindful is breathing.

MINDFULNESS SKILLS

There are a number of fairly simple ways to begin to develop the skill of mindfulness. However, just because they are simple doesn't mean they are easy. As with any skill, they demand practice and continual attention. There is no certificate of completion with regard to mindfulness. Attention to this practice keeps it alive.

The Relaxation Response

In the 1960s, Herbert Benson, a Harvard medical researcher, was able to train monkeys to raise and lower their blood pressure simply by turning on different colored lights. His findings intrigued practitioners of transcendental meditation (TM), who believed that their form of meditation lowered blood pressure, although they had no way to prove it. After much prompting, Benson agreed to set up a series of experiments. They were right; TM did lower blood pressure. Based on these findings, Benson began to study this phenomenon.

To move away from the spiritually-based practice of TM, he devised a simple process in which the subject of the experiment simply repeated the word "one" for a period of time. The results were similar to those achieved by TM practitioners.

In the new edition of *The Relaxation Response*, Benson and his colleagues found that favorable results depend on only two things:

1. A mental device, such as a sound, word, phrase, or prayer repeated silently or aloud or a fixed gaze at an object.
2. A passive attitude — not worrying about how well one is performing the technique and simply putting aside any distracting thoughts to return to one's focus.[2]

They found that these conditions could be met anywhere, while seated or while moving. In the tests with TM meditators, they found that the drop in blood pressure did not occur during the meditation practice itself, but occurred as a result of repeated practice.

This book is not about changing your blood pressure as such, but blood pressure certainly can be an indicator of tension.

Benson's approach is a good way to learn to remain calm while remaining engaged. The relaxation response practice increases alpha wave activity in the brain, which allows us to be calm and alert at the same time. Practices such as the Relaxation Response can help us dissipate the power of knee-jerk reactions more quickly.

The Lost Art of Breathing

What could be simpler than breathing? It's an involuntary act. No baby has to be taught how to breathe. They just do it. But when we are tense we hold our breath or our breathing becomes very shallow. This constriction is muscle tension, which deprives the brain of oxygen.

Breathing is a fundamental skill taught in martial arts, meditation, stress reduction, sports, music, and acting. Sadly, it is not taught in many business schools or sales courses.

Counting Your Breaths

This is a deceptively simple exercise. All you do is count your breaths while paying attention.

1. Sit.
2. Allow your muscles to relax so you are sitting comfortably. I don't recommend doing this lying down, as it is very easy to fall asleep in a prone position.
3. Without straining, take a deep breath, paying attention to the air coming in.
4. Hold your breath for a moment.
5. Exhale slowly. If you inhaled on four counts, try to exhale on eight. But don't force the breath. If you can only exhale for five or six counts, that's OK.
6. Try counting to yourself as you inhale: 1 . . . 2 . . . 3 . . . 4. Hold. Count on the exhale: 1 . . . 2 . . . 3 . . . 4 . . . 5 . . . 6 . . . 7 . . . 8.
7. Do the exercise in sets of ten. Ten inhalations, ten exhalations make a set. Begin with one set. Once that feels comfortable, try adding a second and third set to your routine.

Graduate-Level Breathing

Here's a more challenging variation. Breathe in slowly. Hold. Breathe out slowly. As you begin, think "one." On the second round, think "two," and so on. As soon as you notice that your attention wanes for even a moment, begin again with round one.

In these exercises, try to accept the fact that you may drift in and out of awareness. If you begin to judge yourself for these shifts in attention — or to congratulate yourself for doing so well — you will be pulling yourself further away from the practice. Just notice that you are distracted. Like clouds, these thoughts will pass by if you allow them to.

If you practice any of these exercises daily for fifteen to twenty minutes, I believe you will begin to notice a difference in how you relate to others and in your ability to pay attention to what's going on around you. You will probably find that you are generally calmer and are taking more things in stride.

Brain research shows that looking at a situation without judgment — simply being mindful of what is going on — can in itself transform negative emotions into positive ones. Without resorting to *Little Engine That Could* tricks like saying, "I think I can. I think I can," our brain releases the hold the negative had on us.[3]

Focus on Your Center of Gravity

A spot about two inches below your navel is thought to be your center of gravity. Practitioners of the Chinese martial art T'ai Chi practice putting their attention in this spot. If you do this exercise, you'll probably begin to feel that you are standing in a way that is well-supported, as if you were deeply rooted into the ground. T'ai Chi practitioners use this exercise to learn to keep their center of gravity low. This allows them to move without being thrown off balance so easily.

Skeptical? Try this simple exercise. Stand and imagine your center of gravity being in your forehead. Ask a friend to push one of your shoulders. Try it again with your center of gravity in your chest. And a third time imagining your center of gravity two inches below your navel. Don't stand rigidly, but allow yourself to move with the push while keeping your feet stationary. Most people find that they are toppled easily when their center of gravity is high. When their center is low, they tend to have a broader range of motion while staying in balance. Here is a way to focus on your center:

1. Stand with feet about shoulder-width apart.
2. Imagine a plumb line dropping from your center to the floor.
3. As you breathe in slowly, imagine the air moving down into your center.
4. As you exhale slowly, imagine the air is moving down through your legs and feet and into the ground.
5. Repeat for at least a few minutes.

If you begin to feel tension in any part of your body that distracts you, just allow yourself to relax in that area and refocus on your center. This approach to focusing on your center can be helpful before going into a meeting — and, if you're subtle, during meetings themselves.

OTHER WAYS TO PREPARE

Increasing our ability to be mindful is the most effective resource we have. Staying mindful — calm and alert without judgment — allows us to draw on the full range of our skills. When we can combine our skills with mindfulness, we have a powerful combination. Here are some ways to increase skills when engaging others:

Rehearse to Break Habitual Responses
Rehearsing in the right manner can be a powerful way to support yourself. In a workshop, I was coaching Darrell on a problem he was having at work. He was stuck. He always responded the same way when he worked with his co-worker. As he saw it, he had no options. I asked him to play it as a scene to show us what the situation typically looked like. I watched as he and the other "actor" worked. Almost immediately his partner was able to make Darrell respond with an aggressive knee-jerk reaction. I stopped the scene and asked him to try it again and do something different. Not better, just different. I didn't want him to get stuck thinking about the right way to do it. I simply wanted him to break out of his rut.

The scene started. His partner said a line that caused him to react. Darrell stopped for a moment, not sure what to do next, and then burst out laughing. This was an unusual response, but very liberating for him. But we didn't stop there. Without analyzing how well he did, I asked him to try it a third way. Once again, I wasn't interested in seeing him do it right. I just wanted him to experiment with playing the scene differently. On the third round, he growled.

This may sound odd to you. I am not suggesting to Darrell or you that you actually laugh or growl in front of co-workers. I simply wanted him (and you) to see that he had options. Once you begin to break a habit, you can begin to explore options that might include some of the skills discussed in this book.

A good way to figure out what to rehearse is to pay attention to your knee-jerk reactions. Ask yourself, "What knee-jerk reactions am I likely to use with him or her?" "What triggers those reactions?" And then play with options. The first step is to break out of a calcified, habitual pattern, so I encourage you to stay away from just rehearsing what you believe the right way is. Like Darrell, just try out some new stuff.

Find Your Achilles' Heel

In *Impro*, Keith Johnstone writes, "It is important for an actor to accept being insulted. The stage becomes an even more 'dangerous' area if you can't accept your disabilities."[4] He suggests that actors will never feel safe until they allow themselves to accept the parts of themselves they fear others will see. Sometimes our knee jerks come from the fear that people will see something in us that we prefer stay covered up. Fact is, those things we want to keep hidden usually are plain for all to see.

Knowing what it is you are afraid others will see can relieve some of the potential sting. Often it is the fear that they will say something that gives their words the power to keep us off balance. While there is no easy way to accept these parts of ourselves, the repetition that comes from rehearsal can help.

Another way to begin to look at these fears is to expand on the mindfulness exercises covered earlier in this chapter in the following ways:

1. Use one of the exercises to relax into a calm and alert state. Many believe that it takes about fifteen minutes for us to slow down so that we are focusing easily on our breathing.

2. Imagine something the other person could say that might set you off. Just notice how you react. Pay attention to any thoughts that come to mind. Notice any physical reactions. Try not to judge these reactions, just notice them. Imagine you are able to look at the situation from various vantage points. Notice what the scene looks like from these various viewpoints. If you begin to judge or to problem solve, just allow those thoughts to pass and continue to notice.

3. You may begin to see the power of the emotional charge dissipate to some degree. If that occurs, great. If not, try not to judge yourself or the exercise. Just notice what's going on.

Use a Coach

A coach can be a good resource for helping you stay calm when working with others. Your coach needn't be a professional; a friend who likes you and has a reasonable degree of interpersonal skills will do nicely.

Like a sports coach, your coach can help you before the big game. Unlike a sports coach, he won't be running up and down the sidelines as you play or throw chairs at you when you mess up. The coach's role is to help you. Here are some of the functions coaches can perform:

- **Heighten awareness.** Your coach can help you see what you're missing. Daniel was concerned that his son was not going to be placed in a program he believed his son deserved. Daniel feared that he would be seen as just another one of those demanding parents, so was reluctant to talk with the teacher. Daniel talked with his coach about it. The coach pointed out that Daniel was painting this as a win-lose confrontation when, in fact, he had a good relationship with his son's teacher. His coach suggested that he enter the conversation with the teacher as an exploration, without making any demands. Daniel's facial muscles relaxed. That's all he needed. He had the skills to hold a good conversation, but he had created a picture that wouldn't allow him to use those skills. The exchange with the coach took less than five minutes as they were driving to a meeting.

- **Practice.** Your coach can practice with you. She can play the other person in the exchange. Or if you really want to make it interesting, ask your coach to play you. This allows you to step into the shoes of the other person. That step alone can be very beneficial as you begin to see yourself through another's eyes. After practicing you can debrief. What worked? What didn't? Where did you revert to a knee-jerk reaction? What could you do differently?

- **Have fun with the practice.** Stop the scene and rewind and try things again. Don't assume there is only one right way to do something. Try out a variety of approaches just to see what might happen.

- **See patterns.** If you work with your coach over a period of time, she can begin to see patterns in how you work with others. She can warn you of trouble ahead. Janice often calls on her colleague, Ruth Ann, for coaching assistance. In one such meeting, Janice talked about how she was going to confront her boss for not keeping commitments. As Ruth Ann listened, she heard one of Janice's patterns. Janice tended to be wishy-washy when she believed she was actually confronting. Ruth Ann pointed this out to her. Now Janice had options. She could go in with her timeworn, wishy-washy approach or she could try a stronger, assertive approach.

  Recognition of our patterns allows us to see how we habitually respond — and that can give us the freedom to explore other options.

- **Regain composure.** Just by talking with you — and especially from listening to you — your coach can help you settle down. Just as the power of paying attention is effective when we are trying to influence someone else, these same skills can be used by your coach to support you.

- **Analyze encounters.** As dispassionately as possible, dissect exchanges: he said, she said. Look for key moments and turning points.

- **Give advice.** I put this idea last for emphasis, because even when we ask for advice, it is often hard to take it. You're still struggling with what went wrong (or could go wrong), and your coach is telling you what to do. Many times we resist the very advice we ask for and we employ one of our knee-jerk reactions. We explain and defend. We grow quiet. We seethe. We make false promises. You say, "Thanks, Jeff, that was very helpful. I'll consider your suggestions seriously." But you are really thinking, "Yeah, right, not in this lifetime."

Debrief Yourself

Books and workshops are fine ways to begin to learn a new skill, but they don't go far enough. The only way to really learn a skill is to practice in encounters with others and then reflect afterwards on what happened. Sports teams watch game films; symphonies rehearse. People in business just go from event to event, with hardly a breath or a thought about why they were successful today and yesterday they recreated Mount St. Helen's in the boardroom.

A technique I learned many years ago goes by the acronym IAG — identify, analyze, and generalize.[5] The basic steps are:

- **I — Identify.** First, identify the particular portions of the meeting that you want to debrief. These should be troubling moments or times when things started to shift for the better. Debrief each moment separately.
- **A — Analyze.** What happened at each moment in the exchange? Try to do this without judgment. Think of it as a rational analysis of the event: When I said X, she responded with Z.
- **G — Generalize.** What can you learn from this analysis that you can apply when you meet this person again? What can you generalize that you could use when you want to influence other people?

You can find step-by-step details for IAG on my Website at www.beyondresistance.com.

Support Yourself during the Exchange

During the conversation, nervousness can limit your ability to use the skills you have. You hear yourself saying things you wish you hadn't said or you just forget to make certain points. Here are some ideas that can help you stay calm and engaged in real time.

Let Go of What You Know

If you've been reading this book closely, you may be swimming in a mess of good intentions. So many things to remember. In one of Bob Hope's comedies, he thinks he is a gunslinger.[6] The villain challenges him to a gunfight, which he accepts. Everyone except Hope knows that he will be in serious trouble. As he walks out of the bar, a guy pulls him aside and tells him that the wind is from the west, so lean to the east. Another tells him that the bad guy is tall, so crouch down low. Still another suggests that he dodge and move kind of quickly. By the time he reaches the street,

Staying calm to stay engaged is the opposite of a knee-jerk reaction. The other side of the issues that cause our knees to jerk (Level 2 and 3 issues) are the ones that can help us remain calm.

he is filled with way too many good intentions. He can't keep it all in his head, much less make use of any of this advice. You may be feeling the same way.

To watch Laura Linney and Mark Ruffalo in the movie *You Can Count on Me* is to watch two masters at work. In each moment they respond to each other as if they are actually brother or sister talking. They respond with all the complex history that goes into many adult sibling relationships. Writer and director of the film Kenneth Lonergan explained, "They are available to each other." In an interview with Charlie Rose, the actors talked about how they do their jobs. Both do significant preparation before ever walking on the set. They know their characters and how they relate to others in the film. They know their characters' history, shining moments, and foibles. They "take every concept of how a scene should go," Ruffalo said, and then let it go. "You do a ton of work," said Linney, "and throw it out the window."[7]

For Linney and Ruffalo, letting go of what they know is as if all that preparation work goes into resident memory so that they can be fully attentive to their partners. This allows them to be surprised and responsive without faking it. In applying the principles of engagement, once we've established our intention, considered the context, thought about how we might pay attention without resorting to knee-jerk responses, it's time to let the preparation go and meet the other person.

Of course, this is easier said than done. I believe we hang onto what we know because we are afraid of letting go. Actors take comfort in knowing their lines. Executives in the gee-whiz glitz of their slideshow presentations replete with moving graphics. Salespeople in the stock comebacks to objections made by prospects. Parents to the status that they believe should come from being the mommy or the daddy. None of these allows us to meet the other person fully.

A client told me that when he faced a tough meeting with his boss, "I was more wedded to my behavior than I was to my intention." My client didn't need more skills. He was top-heavy with skills. He needed to be able to relax a bit so he could use what he knew. Knowing his own knee-jerk reactions was a good start, but he needed a way to keep his intention in mind while in the midst of these conversations.

Put Things in Perspective

Just before a performance, the legendary orchestra conductor Arturo Toscanini and the cellist Gregor Piatigorsky were standing in the wings of the concert hall. One asked the other, "How are you feeling?" The other answered, "Terrible, because I'm no good." The first one replied, "I'm not any good either, but we're no worse than the rest of them. Let's go."[8] Almost everyone has doubts. Holding our fears lightly can often release their power to overwhelm us.

MINDFULNESS IN THE MOMENT

The benefit from all the mindfulness exercises is cumulative. You will probably begin to note how you approach people and events a bit differently after you've practiced any of these for a while. In addition, it can be helpful to have ways to return to a mindful non-judgmental state when you are engaged in conversation with another person.

One way to be mindful is to pay attention to your physical reactions while you are with another person. Physical shifts occur involuntarily and can be a quick signal that you are beginning to tense.

Since your body goes with you wherever you go, and it reacts all the time, you might practice paying attention to your physical reactions in situations where little is at stake. For example, when you are on hold with your credit card company waiting for someone to come on the line. Or when you meet an old friend and are just catching up. In other words, you can play with it when the stakes are low.

A Game Plan

Create an agenda for the conversation. You might consider using a one-page sheet that lists the points you'd like to explore. The document is something that both of you can follow. It is not your secret little game plan.

"Bill, I appreciate you taking time to meet with me regarding computer systems. Here is a sheet that has the four points I'd like us to explore.

- My case for why we need a new computer system
- Your thoughts regarding a system
- Explore any major differences
- See whether it's possible for us to agree on a solution

"Anything you'd add to that agenda? OK then, let's get started."

You'll note that the agenda is created in such a way that you can be open to being influenced, even in the opening moments of the conversation. This expansive spirit can set the tone for the meeting. Without explicitly saying it, you are signaling that you wish to approach the conversation in an I/You manner.

Breathing

Remember to breathe. As you feel tension mounting — for example, muscles constricting — allow yourself to breathe deeply. You might try breathing through your nose. People tend to breathe more deeply when they inhale through their noses.

Three-Point Check

Here is a simple tool that you can use anywhere. Just the simple act of noticing where you are tense often reduces the tension to some degree. There are three points that I find particularly important: my jaw, my shoulders, and my lower back. Your most critical three points may differ from mine.

Place your attention on your jaw and notice whether it's tense or relaxed. If it is tense, allow your muscles to relax. If they don't let go, don't fight it, just move on. Turn your attention to your shoulders and do the same thing. Finally, focus on your lower back and repeat the same process. Once you get used to it, you probably will be able to complete the three-point check in a few seconds.

You can use the technique repeatedly throughout a meeting. It's fast and nobody knows you're doing it. As far as anyone can tell, you're just a normal businessperson. Little do they know that you are equipped with this advanced, esoteric, touchy-feely skill.

Take a Break

As I mentioned in the chapter on knee-jerk reactions, breaks are wonderful. Here are a few additional thoughts about them. If it weren't for the finite capacity of human bladders, I think some business meetings I've been in would still be going on. Breaks allow us to break out of habits that aren't serving us. Get up. Walk across the room. Get something to drink. Walk outside. Do anything except continue the conversation. This can help revitalize both of you.

Breaks allow us to literally break out of our habitual patterns. When people know each other well, they may find themselves playing out a well-rehearsed drama. The script was written long ago. You can almost predict what you and the other person will say next, and yet you seem powerless to stop the tragedy. A break in the action allows you to consider what you're doing and to try something different.

It only takes one person to change his or her part of the play for the entire script to change.

How do you know you need to take a break?

- You hear yourself or the other person saying the same thing over and over again.
- You're not listening or the other person isn't listening.
- You can't pull back from one of your knee-jerk reactions.

- The other person seems very upset by this exchange, and you are unable to reduce the Level 2 or Level 3 tension.

MOVING AHEAD

It was 10 p.m. and my delayed flight had just arrived at O'Hare Field. I saw that my connecting flight to Champaign-Urbana had been cancelled. I pulled out my flight guide and saw that it had been the last flight out for the day. I could feel my heart begin to race. I had to be in Champaign the next morning to give a speech. I ran over to a gate agent who simply didn't have time for me. She waved me down the hall to another agent. As I walked the hundred feet or so to the next agent, I continued to walk fast, but I slowed down inside. I took deeper breaths. I noticed tension in my shoulder. Just noticing the tension allowed my muscles to relax some. In those moments I became less desperate. I started to see options I could explore and questions I could ask the agent. I could check on flights on other airlines. See if there was a shuttle that ran to that city. See if they would reimburse the cost of a rental car (which they did). All of these options occurred quickly simply because I slowed down.

The more you practice the simple techniques described here, the more natural they will feel and the more easily you'll be able to draw on them when you are in potentially tense situations.

CHAPTER 11

Ways to Avoid Resistance in the First Place

When a patient says, "You don't understand," and I think I do, I'm wrong.
— Gary Yontef, clinical psychologist and author

When I first met Sarah, she worked in a research lab and hated her job. Soon she took a new job down the hall. The pay was the same. She had the same parking spot. The type of work itself was no more interesting than her last assignment. Even the swill that passed for coffee was the same. And yet, when I asked about her new job, she said, "I love it."

Sarah told me that the difference was her new boss. He was available. She said that he sort of "hung out" in the hallway. There was a spot where the two hallways intersected, and during the course of the day everyone walked by it a few times. He stood there with coffee cup in hand. As people walked by, he struck up brief conversations. Often, as an employee made another run past this spot, the boss would have new information that would help. He might say, "I talked with Jim about that problem you mentioned, and I think we can do something about it."

He got things done by hanging out and being available for conversation. But even more important, he built relationships so things could get done. Sarah trusted him and had confidence in his leadership.

THE STRUGGLE

Resistance to an idea is a good thing. It suggests that people feel strongly about the issue. It allows us to hear information that could save us time, money, or even embarrassment. That's why the principles Explore Deeply and Find Ways to Connect are so important. But when people don't know us or trust us, they may be more inclined to resist without giving us the benefit of the doubt. Opposition that is born of fear takes over. That resistance can be harmful and overshadow any possible excitement. It is a reaction against our idea or against us and may have nothing to do with what they think of the idea itself.

The best way to increase the odds that people will accept your ideas is to create an atmosphere in which there is little Level 2 or Level 3 resistance in the first place. The way to do this is to build stronger relationships. People are less likely to seriously resist a person whom they like and trust. In other words, the better the relationship, the less likely you will be faced with deep resistance. People may still disagree with your ideas and decisions, but without the strong emotion and fear that go with more intense forms of resistance. And when deep resistance does arise from natural fear of change, a strong relationship gives you a foundation for exploring differences.

Why the Obvious Isn't So Obvious
You probably didn't reach for the yellow highlighter as you read that last paragraph. The value of building strong relationships is probably not earth-shattering news to you. But, here's the problem: Although most of us know that strong relationships are important, we don't spend much time developing them. It is important to examine what stops us from doing what we know is important.

We Value Transactions over Connections
The United States is a transaction-based culture. We want what we want when we want it — and that means now! I buy my shirts by calling an 800 number. The company keeps my size and item number on file. I simply give my credit card number and tell them how many shirts I want. Then I hang up. The customer service rep and I don't chat about kids, weather,

football, springtime in Wisconsin, or anything else for that matter. We only talk about shirts and money, and I like it that way.

But when you want to influence someone else, relationships are critical. People are more likely to go along with someone they like. They will give people they like the benefit of any doubt. They are likely to listen longer to someone they like. Building relationships increases the social capital. Without this good will, people are limited to paying attention to just the merits of your ideas as they perceive them — and the stories they make up about who you are and what you're really looking for. Those are big hurdles to overcome.

Good salespeople will tell you that repeat business is the foundation of their success. Customers are more inclined to consider new products and services from someone they believe treated them well in the past. A transaction-based mentality works fine when you're buying shirts, but use that same style in the workplace or home, and you have problems.

What if the only time you talk with the kids is when you want them to do something important, like stay in school and graduate? What if the only time the people in the accounting department see you is when you want them to cut you some slack and simplify a reporting procedure? What if most of your exchanges with your spouse are over the day-to-day minutia of who will pick up the dry cleaning or take the car in for service, but now you want to discuss raiding the retirement fund to buy a boat or quitting your job to start a new business? These simple transactions don't build the solid foundation necessary to handle the struggles of deeper resistance.

Transaction-based exchanges are based on simple reciprocity. You scratch my back, I'll scratch yours. I give the clothing company money, they send me shirts. As long as we limit what we want from each other to shirts and money, the transaction works fine. But much of our lives is not that neat and simple. If so, you wouldn't be reading this book.

Ron was head of a department in a medical supply company. His staff hardly knew him because most contact was limited to transactions where he did most of the talking. Individual and group meetings were efficient, functional affairs. There was an agenda, and when it was completed the meeting was over. If Ron called, you knew he wanted something from you. People often went along with these requests

IDEAS FOR BUILDING STRONGER RELATIONSHIPS

Here are some ideas that work:

- **Manage by wandering around.** Tom Peters and Robert Waterman coined this term in their classic book *In Search of Excellence*. They simply meant that managers should spend more unscheduled time being available. Wandering around the halls, the copy room, conference areas. Hanging out in the lunchroom or cafeteria. Leaning against a wall with a cup of coffee in hand counts too. Don't set an agenda for your walks, just appear. And do it often. The first time you venture out of your cocoon, people will be suspicious: "What's she up to?" "He must have just read another self-help book." "Whatever you do, don't look up." This cynicism will pass if you are persistent. Within a short time, people will begin to pull you aside to ask or tell you things. This begins building the relationships you need.
- **Go to lunch.** Take people to lunch, either one on one or in small groups. This makes you available for all manner of conversations.
- **Give yourself extra time before and after staff meetings for people to pull you aside.** If you are available, people will talk to you. By arriving at the meeting a few minutes early, you invite informal, relaxed conversation. Woody Allen once said that 80 percent of success is just showing up. So increase your percentage and show up early.
- **Ask for advice from your staff.** Scott is a senior manager in an insurance company. He said that pulling people together to critique his work did a significant amount to build trust in his office. Soon people were bringing their own projects to the group for critique. He had launched a process that allowed people to let down their guard because he had done so first.
- **Use what you've learned.** Most important, use the six principles to begin building the relationships that ultimately will build support for your new ideas.

because they wanted to keep their jobs, not because they liked his ideas. If they liked an idea, they would give it 100 percent commitment; if they didn't, they would do just enough to keep Ron off their backs. There is a big difference between the quality of work that comes from commitment versus compliance.

Because there was no give-and-take relationship between Ron and his staff, no one ever found out why some of these ideas were important to him, nor did they care. If Ron had been better at building solid working relationships, people might have been interested in his thinking and made some effort to make the ideas come alive.

When relationships are merely transactions with others, people have little reason to say yes. We make it easy for people to dismiss us and our ideas. Consequently, people may not take time to even consider the merits of our ideas.

We Believe Relationships Will Take Care of Themselves

What we say we believe and how we act are not always the same thing. While many would say that relationships are critical to being able to influence someone else, their actions say something different. Their behavior says that efficiency or financial outcomes are their gods.

Ted was vice-president at the headquarters of a bank. A major part of his job was ensuring that headquarters and the branch offices worked together. Since the branches had a fair amount of autonomy, this could be a challenge at times. Often, branches saw corporate as a group that got in the way of good work. Headquarters held a similar view of the branches. Ted walked into a Level 3 situation, where history and trust were big issues, and he was supposed to build bridges.

He stepped into this position knowing the difficulty he faced. In fact, he knew that the Level 3 animosity had nothing to do with him or his arrival on the scene. Even though he met frequently with the branches, they continued to distrust him and what he represented.

The Level 3 issue of trust and mistrust is the foundation for work and personal relationships. This area often gets far too little meaningful attention in the workplace.

Ted was organized and held efficient businesslike meetings. He thought they would appreciate this concern for their time. They probably did, but his bullet-point style did little to change their perception of him. He seemed to believe that talent, commitment to corporate goals, and hard work were enough. As important as those things are, they are seldom enough in situations like Ted's. He was doomed from the start. He eventually lost his job, not for lack of talent or commitment, but because he never took the Level 3 issues seriously.

We Believe That Relationships Are for Wimps

Another belief that can get in the way is the belief that relationships are for the weak. We seem to think because John Wayne could clean up the town alone, so can we.

In the United States and many other countries, attention to relationships takes on a strong gender bias. Men aren't supposed to pay attention to those soft, touchy-feely issues. The underlying belief may be, "I'll look foolish. The guys will see me as soft." There are so many corporate cultures run by white guys that women, people of color, and those from different cultures often learn to play by the same white-guy rules.

Examining Beliefs

None of the ideas in this chapter matters if you don't believe relationships are important to your success. In other words, using good tools with the wrong intention will probably fail. Playing at an I/You intention, when what you believe in is I/It, won't work. I've seen managers hold team feedback sessions, because it seemed like the thing to do, and harm working relationships because they reacted strongly when anyone actually gave them feedback. I've seen other managers try to give and receive feedback with little grace or skill, and the session went well simply because they truly wanted to engage in that process.

If you're skeptical, you might try an experiment. Identify a few times when you've been wildly successful in getting others excited about your ideas. And identify

Your belief about relationships is a far better predictor of success than any tips you could get from this book.

some times when you've been unsuccessful getting others to accept your ideas. Look at both sets of responses through the lens of relationships. You will probably find that your success was greater when you enjoyed a strong working relationship with others.

WHERE ARE YOU?

Some cultures, including some within the United States, are more relationship-based. In these cultures, relationship is key to doing business. Part of any exchange — even at work — includes asking about the kids, talking about the weather, or showing deep concern for the fate of a favorite local sports team. In Turkey, for example, it is common to have tea in the course of business transactions. In many banks and shops, you are offered tea. This is quite different from our transaction-based ATM culture, where the exchange is between a machine and us. Put card in, take money out. I and It.

How can you tell whether your contact is based on transactions or on relationship? Here's a checklist to start you thinking about it. Some telling features of transaction-based exchanges are:

- The exchange is limited to a specific request and response.
    Will you take in the mail for us?
    Do you still want those white shirts in 16 × 32?
    Do you want fries with that?
- The exchange cannot move easily beyond the confines of the current transaction. I like the letter carrier who delivers our mail, but our conversations never venture far from letters and packages. It would be inappropriate to discuss politics in an effort to enlist her support for a candidate, or to ask her to sign a petition.
- When one side makes a big request, the exchange turns into a poker game. Both sides play their cards close to the vest, giving out only minimal bits of information. This limited relationship cannot bear the weight of heavier requests.
- At work, you limit your involvement with others to business-related matters only.

People in service professions such as consultants, lawyers, and accountants think in terms of billable hours. Nothing wrong with this, except that you risk turning yourself into a commodity, and that makes it easier for people to move on when they find someone else who can fulfill your end of the transaction. Parents who think in terms of "quality time" run the risk of reducing their time with children to transactions. "Whew! I put in my two hours with the little brat for another week." Spouses who keep score also operate in this way. "We spent five long days at your parents' house last year. This year we're spending the holidays with mine. What's fair is fair."

Here are some important features of relationship-based exchanges:

- The quality of the exchange is relatively easy. You can speak to each other without worrying about saying something the wrong way. When you do disagree strongly, the relationship can handle the conflict.
- You value the exchange between you. You are interested in your own wishes and needs *and* in the needs of the other person. In other words, you seem to work naturally toward an I/You relationship.
- At work, you actually look for time to spend together that isn't "billable." You may spend time talking about things that aren't business related. You can laugh together.
- You know more about the people involved. With your neighbors, you know something about their interests. At work, you understand and appreciate the challenges co-workers face and know what excites them.

Excitement Is the Biggest Challenge

Just because you spend time together doesn't guarantee you will be able to communicate better or agree more often, but it sure increases the odds in your favor. Also, building stronger relationships tends to be a more satisfying way for most of us to get through life. It adds a richness and depth that mere transactions can't give us.

Of course there are some, perhaps many, who prefer "doing the deal" to anything else. In their eyes, relationships only slow people down. History is full of examples that failed miserably primarily because people saw everything as a series of transactions. Getting excited about doing the deal happens every day at every level of the organization (and it occurs at home as well). People get excited about their idea and forget about the people who must accept it.

REPAIRING LEVEL 3 RELATIONSHIPS

When your relationship is in the midst of Level 3 mistrust, it may be close to impossible to put forward any idea until you begin to increase trust. Fear of who you are and what you may represent stands in the way of people hearing or believing you.

The challenge of Level 3 is that there is no easy way out. At times you may feel you are taking one step forward and two steps back. Progress can be slow, and the least little thing can set it back. Look at the tension between Israelis and Palestinians. It takes very little provocation to undo agreements. Suspicions are so high and the animosities so old that trust can seem naïve.

Knowing that there is no foolproof approach, here are some things that can help.

A Firm Belief in I and You

If I want to build a relationship just so I can get something (an It), people may go along if they see that the It is in their interests as well. But Level 3 relationship situations can be so tense that sometimes it is only our commitment to stick with the other person that allows any hope of progress.

While it is possible that I will never be able to repair the Level 3 damage adequately, I must believe that I can, or I will give up long before I ever know whether success is possible. I must be able to look at you and see a human who has values, wishes, and dreams just like I do.

Make the First Move

Extend an olive branch. People often wait for others to make the first move. Pride often gets in the way. Vera was estranged from her son. They hadn't spoken in years. When she turned sixty, she called him and suggested meeting for coffee. They met. One brief visit turned into another and another. Over time, they found that, whatever the past problems had been, they could be put behind them. Today, their relationship is pretty strong. And Vera gets to be a doting grandmother.

It is the small first steps that get things started.

Find Common Concerns

John Sweeney, head of the AFL-CIO, would meet with corporate leaders to look at common concerns. These meetings had nothing to do with any ongoing negotiations. They were simply an opportunity to discuss issues of interest to both parties. Those meetings were significantly different from traditional antagonistic relationships between management and labor. His gesture was only a small step, and that's its beauty.

Sometimes people can come together to tackle issues of common concern. In some cities, pro-life and pro-choice advocates have worked together to address issues of unwanted teen pregnancy. If these people can work together — given the strength of their Level 3 value differences — then it certainly seems that there is a way to find common ground on most of the Level 3 issues that occur in the workplace.

Keep Commitments

People liked Brad but didn't respect him. He didn't seem to be serious about his job. They couldn't trust him. Then he made a significant change in his behavior. He began to keep his word. If he made a promise to do something, he did it. And he was careful to make only promises he knew he could keep. Over the course of about six months, people's perception of him changed. They started asking him to take part in key assignments. Brad never saw himself as unreliable, but he realized that others viewed him that way — and that those perceptions were all that mattered if he wanted to increase his influence.

Similarly, acting consistently in ways that appear worthy of trust makes a difference. Claudia was a music teacher and went from class to class, so she could come and go as she pleased. She would even leave the building for lunch. Technically, this was OK, but none of the other teachers had the freedom to leave the building. For them, staying in at lunch was a commitment that everyone should make. She never recognized that her actions were seen as arrogant. Consequently, when

HOW YOU CAN TELL WHEN
RELATIONSHIPS ARE WORKING

Look at the list of people you have identified as important to your success. Rate your relationship with each of them using the following assessment. Think about one individual (or group) as you complete it.

1. People volunteer information about their beliefs, values, and concerns to you.

1	2	3	4	5
Not at all		Somewhat		To a significant degree

2. Few topics seem to be off-limits in your conversations with this person.

1	2	3	4	5
Not at all		Somewhat		To a significant degree

3. You feel free to say just about anything to this person. You don't spend lots of time rehearsing every sentence, worried about how things will come out of your mouth.

1	2	3	4	5
Not at all		Somewhat		To a significant degree

4. You laugh together. Not just telling jokes, but there is a lightness of spirit between you.

1	2	3	4	5
Not at all		Somewhat		To a significant degree

5. It is enjoyable to be together. You look forward to spending time with this person.

1	2	3	4	5
Not at all		Somewhat		To a significant degree

6. It is easy to have eye contact with each other. Even given that cultures differ in what constitutes appropriate eye contact, the relationship feels natural. You're not wondering, "Am I doing this right?"

1	2	3	4	5
Not at all		Somewhat		To a significant degree

7. This person is interested in hearing your point of view.

1	2	3	4	5
Not at all		Somewhat		To a significant degree

8. You are interested in hearing this person's point of view.

1	2	3	4	5
Not at all		Somewhat		To a significant degree

9. Your digestive system functions normally when you think about this person.

1	2	3	4	5
Not at all		Somewhat		To a significant degree

SCORING

High scores (mostly 4s and 5s): You probably have a very strong relationship that allows you to explore tough issues with few Level 2 or Level 3 disconnects.

Mixed Scores (some high, some low, some mid-range): There may be certain issues that are just too hot for you to handle. When you do try to discuss them, listening breaks down. Take it slow. Pay special attention to the more personal areas where you can talk. Take these exchanges seriously. Building ground on the safer issues makes it safe to begin treading on less-firm soil.

Low scores: You need to decide whether or not this relationship is worth the effort. If so, get to work. This relationship is not going to change just because you wish it would. It will be up to you to begin making changes, at a pace that feels safe.

1. Look at those relationships where you score high and identify the reasons why. Try to be as specific as possible.
2. Using the list you just created and the list of "how to" items included in this chapter, identify a few things you could do to begin to improve the relationship.
3. Don't expect magical results. Relationships turn sour for a reason. They usually don't turn around instantly, but if this person is important to you, you have to try.

she needed their support — say to pull students from class for a special project — they were less inclined to go along.

Mea Culpa

Sincerely accepting responsibility for our actions can be a powerful force. Our own fears about losing face or power or control often get in the way of even seeing that we are part of the problem.

People make a common mistake when taking responsibility: They expect the other person to reciprocate. If they do, that's fine, but that should not be the goal. Mea culpa suggests that we take responsibility — without any expectation that the other person will do the same.

By taking responsibility you are creating a shift in the relationship. Even if the other person does nothing different in that moment, your mea culpa has shaken up the status quo.

Forgive Them

Marietta Jaeger is founder of Murder Victims' Families for Reconciliation. Her young daughter was brutally murdered in 1973. A year later the murderer called at 3 a.m. to taunt her. Jaeger's response was unusual. She asked, "What can I do to help you?" The murderer began to weep and over the course of the call dropped enough clues so the FBI could find him.

Jaeger said, "In the beginning, I would have been happy to kill this man with my bare hands — and could have done it with a smile on my face. That's a normal, valid human response. But I recognized that kind of hatred would undo me. It was not easy. People who think forgiveness is for wimps haven't tried it."[1]

After the fall of apartheid, few would have argued against blacks seeking justice and retribution. But leaders took a different approach; they established the South African Truth Commission. People would be forgiven if they came forward. What's most important about this story is that the black leaders themselves were willing to lead the way by demonstrating that they could forgive their former enemies.

Turn Your Cards Face Up

Open book management is a tool used in some organizations to give everyone access to information on how the business is run. People receive information on trends, opportunities, threats, and financial data. These open books often unleash creativity as people begin to look for ways to save money and seek out ways to tackle problems. Instead of resistance to change, the organization's leaders find people pushing change. When the CEO of a hospital announced that he thought they should create new clinical pathways (something that often makes medical practitioners apoplectic), people said, "It's about time."

Giving people information works one to one. It sometimes takes a while for them to trust that what you're offering is really accurate. With both of you interested in the same information, you increase the likelihood that you'll start to see ways you could work together that would benefit both of you.

Find Opportunities to Listen
When Peter Johnson took over as head of Bonneville Electric Power, environmental groups hated BEP. One of the first things he did was convene meetings with environmental leaders just so he could listen. He said, "People weren't sure I understood their point of view and, more than not, I probably didn't." He explained that this opened the door to a two-way educational process. He sought ways to come up with win-win solutions. People saw that he was sincere, so when he had to hold firm to a decision, they accepted it.

Johnson became committed to public involvement: "Public involvement is the act of actually interacting and dealing peer to peer. Working across the table with your sleeves rolled up, looking at individuals and groups around the region, and treating them as intellectual equals."[2]

MOVING ON

Trust is difficult to build and easy to destroy. That's life. I believe that keeping our focus on I and on You can help us keep the relationship in mind on an equal footing with our ideas (Its).

INTERVIEW WITH MARIAH BURTON NELSON, author of *The Unburdened Heart*

Mariah Burton Nelson is an author, speaker, and former professional basketball player. In *The Unburdened Heart*, she describes how she was able to forgive a man who had abused her when she was a teenager. Her book rises above her personal story and explores the nature of forgiveness itself. Many times, Level 3 issues remain alive because no one has the capacity or willingness to forgive, and the misery lasts forever. (The last person Dante meets in his journey through the Inferno is a count who is condemned for all eternity to gnaw on the skull of his enemy.)

RM: Why forgive?
MBN: It frees you to go ahead and live the rest of your life. It frees you from the past and frees you from anger and a sense of victimization. As long as you're mad about what happened then, you can't fully appreciate what is happening now or plan for what might happen tomorrow.

RM: I would assume that once you forgave others, you would be freer to make contact with them, and perhaps even influence them.
MBN: Yes, and paradoxically, you might be less interested in influencing them. You're less interested in it and it's more likely to happen. Once we really forgive someone we have less desire to control his or her behavior. Once forgiveness happens, you're simultaneously more compassionate for the other person — that's an essential key to forgiveness — but at the same time you're more detached from them and their behavior.

RM: Would you say that forgiving allows the door to be open for whatever might happen?
MBN: Yes, that's a very practical aspect to it. There are spiritual and emotional aspects too – it just plain feels better, it feels right on a more spiritual level. And it is more likely to lead to some sort of successful partnership.

RM: But what about those situations where someone wants to forgive someone, but they are afraid that this person might do it again?

INTERVIEW WITH MARIAH BURTON NELSON (continued)

MBN: Trust is different from forgiveness. Forgiveness is about opening your heart — often reopening your heart — toward somebody who hurt you or disappointed you. And trust is believing that the person won't hurt you again. Often forgiveness requires a certain level of vigilance and boundary setting. You can forgive and still get divorced. You can forgive and still change the locks.

RM: It's like we bundle forgiveness and trust and reverence and respect together as one merit badge and that limits our ability to just forgive.
MBN: That's right.

RM: You're suggesting that we forgive first and not wait for the other person to show contrition?
MBN: Yes. Often we are under the misguided impression that if only we could change someone else's behavior, then we would forgive them. So we often lay that down as a law: "I'm not going to forgive you until you change." You can sort of hear a parental voice in the background saying, "OK, Jimmy, say you're sorry. OK, Sally. He said he was sorry, now you have to forgive him." It's set up on a contingency plan. They need to get on their knees and grovel and promise to never do it again before we'll forgive them.

RM: Would you talk a little about the five keys you explore in *The Unburdened Heart*?
MBN: Often the keys are in order, but they can cycle around. First is awareness, which is asking honestly what happened, not only on the surface, but how did that person's behavior affect me? Why did it hurt me? Why did it make me angry? Second is validation. Talk to somebody who cares. The very act of being listened to is in itself very healing. I will usually seek somebody out who will say, "I'm so sorry that happened. No wonder that hurt you."

RM: That person could be someone who has no connection to the other person or that incident, like a therapist or a good friend?
MBN: Exactly. Generally, it's better if they don't have a connection to that other person. If they do, you may veer over into gossiping, trying to impugn the reputation of that other person. It's not about

them. This is about you getting validated. The first two keys are about taking care of yourself. How were you hurt? Why were you hurt? The third key is compassion. Begin to ask, Who is that human being? What is going on in their life? What sort of circumstances might have led them to do something that was so hurtful? Then you realize that behind every jerk is a sad story.

RM: There's a title for you — behind every jerk is a sad story!
MBN: *(laughter)* Good idea. Even if you don't know that sad story, you can make it up. You can imagine. Or you can remember your own experience. When you hurt somebody else, you are usually acting out of ignorance or fear or pain of some kind. You can assume that about others. That leads to humility, which is the fourth step: remembering our own faults and failings. When I start to feel angry or self-righteous and say, "Oh, I would never do something like that," it doesn't take long before I remember that I have done something like that or wanted to or almost did or might have done something like that. The last key is self-forgiveness. I think a lot of times when we won't forgive other people it's because we haven't forgiven ourselves for similar kinds of offenses or for other offenses and that self-directed anger gets mirrored out toward other people.

RM: What would you say are the main ways forgiveness can influence others?
MBN: First, when you forgive someone, you release them from the distraction of your anger or bitterness, which makes room for them to resolve their own feelings about what they did. Often your forgiveness will become a catalyst for them to forgive themselves. Second, when you forgive yourself, you become happier, easier to get along with, and hence a more agreeable, productive team player. Self-forgiveness also teaches you about compassion, which you will naturally begin to extend to others, thereby improving the quality of your interactions with them, and even the quality of their lives. And third, if you demonstrate forgiveness and self-forgiveness on a daily basis, it will give your employees, colleagues, friends, and family permission to make mistakes, to take themselves less seriously, and to be relaxed and authentic, rather than fearful and defensive. Your forgiving tone will create an atmosphere of gentleness and acceptance, which can make a work or home environment quite pleasant!

CHAPTER 12

What to Do When the Principles Aren't Enough

If at first you don't succeed, failure may be your style.
— Quentin Crisp, memoirist and self-proclaimed retired waif

The danger with books like this is that a reader can come away with the illusion that the world is simple and predictable. All you have to do is follow a few simple steps, and, voilà, success will be yours. Making easy promises to readers is nothing more than a modern version of snake oil. Although books may give some useful pointers, they can be extremely harmful as well. Consider some of the diet books on the market today that go against all credible research on nutrition and human physiology. These books play off our need to find simple solutions to complex problems.[1]

I built this book around six principles that I believe are sound and can increase the chances of meeting your goals while building stronger relationships. I believe these principles can help keep your attention on ways to ensure that people understand your idea, react favorably to it, and trust you. However, these principles are not magical; they are not a tidy set of linear and foolproof steps; and they certainly don't fit every situation.

In this chapter, I want to differentiate between those times when the principles in this book can serve you well and those times when you'll probably need to try something else.

WHEN TO APPLY THE PRINCIPLES

Here's when the principles can help:

- **Your intention is I/You.** You want to build support for a particular new idea and you care as much or more about the relationship with the other person as you do about the idea.
- **You want to repair a damaged relationship in order to get a project back on track.** Even though the going might be tough, you see that sticking with the other person through the tension of exploring differences is the only way to reach a point at which you can work together amicably again.
- **You believe that taking the time to build stronger relationships will have some lasting benefit.** Even though it might be easier and faster to muscle through your idea, you realize that you will destroy fragile bonds in the process. You recognize that you and the other person will need to work together many times in the future and see that it is really in your own best interests to take the time to build a solid foundation today.

WHEN TO WAIT

There are times when you might do well to wait a bit before presenting your idea. Good poker players know that they will need to sit out hands when the cards make it too risky to bet. The same is true in life.

Here are some reasons you might want to sit out a hand or two:

- **You've just taken over this job and people don't know you.** Perhaps people see you through a Level 3 lens, raising issues of standing, history, or trust. You may happen to be the most recent replacement in a much-despised vice-president position. Whatever you do at first will be looked at with suspicion.
- **You're entering with a clean slate.** People will probably give you a honeymoon with regard to some types of

decisions, but other decisions may cause a Level 2 emotional reaction. For example, as the new head of operations, you can probably shift priorities some, or suggest a new project without much concern. In fact, people may be quite willing to give you the benefit of any doubt and join with you. But if you come in and announce a major reorganization, you may find that it is met with visible and powerful opposition.

- **People have just completed a similar major change.** A federal agency developed five new performance appraisal systems in less than eight years. People were wildly skeptical and cynical when number six was introduced. Perhaps they did need a new system (they certainly needed something!), but the timing was wrong to try to introduce it so close on the failures of five other similar programs. Timing is a critical part of successful change. Whatever your new idea is — no matter how noble and good — if people think "been there, done that," you'll have difficulty building support for it.

- **People are burned out.** Due to some stress in the organization — say going through a merger complete with major downsizing — people may lack the reserves to take on something else. You can tell this as you look around. If the people in your office walk around as if they were at the cast party for *The Night of the Living Dead*, they're probably burned out.

- **People are overextended.** Remember those jugglers who spun plates on variety shows? They kept amazing us as they added yet another plate. But they had the good sense to stop before all the plates came crashing down. If people are spinning too many plates today, your new plate — even if it's tiny and beautiful — simply can't be spun. You might be well advised to wait until conditions are less hectic.

WHEN TO LEAVE

Some people stay in a losing game too long. A real danger of self-help books is that they often imply that you should be able to do whatever it is — get your way, mend relationships, shed pounds, or raise perfect children. When things don't go as planned, you believe that all you need to do is try a little bit harder. The dang⌣ comes from believing that everything is within our control. Therefore, any problems must be our fault. No matter how much you want things to be different or how hard you try, sometimes you can't make things better.

During the late 1920s and early 1930s, the Comedian Harmonists, a German vocal group made up of Jews and Aryans, was a major international sensation. When the Nazi regime decreed that Jews could no longer work with Christians, the Harmonists assumed they were immune due to their worldwide celebrity. They ignored the signs until they were forced to disband in 1935. The Jews were forbidden to perform at all. The Germany they wished to live in and the country that actually existed were two wildly different places.

Sometimes, we need to take a sober look at our surroundings and leave. Some examples:

- **You've done all you can.** You've used all the skills you have and you still lack influence. Perhaps you do lack sufficient skills to get things done effectively in this environment, or perhaps it is a Level 3 situation and people like you simply aren't taken seriously.

  If you are a member of a group that is seen in a severely negative light, you have a hard choice to make. Do you want to keep trying, knowing that there is little chance of conditions changing? Do you want to lie low, hoping that conditions change? Or, do you want to leave and go somewhere more hospitable? These are not attractive choices, but sometimes they are the only games in town.

  Making the choice to stay in a dangerous situation because you see the possibility of something better happening is one thing. Staying in a bad situation because you'd feel guilty leaving or see yourself as long-suffering is another.

- **Your values are threatened and you have no power to change conditions.** In the mid-1990s, Mary Ann worked in a plant in the Midwestern part of the United States. Her boss liked to take the staff out to unwind after work. A nice gesture, but he took them to topless bars. The mostly male staff seemed to enjoy these outings (or at least kept quiet if they were offended). Mary Ann found topless clubs offensive and never felt she could talk with her boss about this issue. She had a hard choice to make. Would she continue to go with the

Making the decision to stay or leave is often a Level 3 trust decision. When Level 3 resistance is in the air, it can be difficult to think clearly enough to make a good decision.

group and keep quiet? Would she make excuses whenever invitations were offered? Would she leave? There was no right answer for her. It was a question of values and necessity. She had to ask herself, "What am I willing to do and at what price to myself?"[2]

- **You are receiving serious threats or abuse.** If you are in a situation that is dangerous and you cannot change things, leave. Too often people in abusive situations believe the abuse is their fault and think: "If I only were a better person" or "If I only tried harder to make it work." That is a dangerous position to take. It fails to consider the reality of the context. There are many times when people do bad things to other people and the victim is not responsible.

- **You're a voice crying in the wilderness.** You continually come up with grand ideas and no one listens. Perhaps you're ahead of your time or maybe you just come up with a lot of bad ideas. If you truly believe that your ideas are sound and they matter to you, perhaps you need to find a place where you are respected for what you offer.

A number of years ago, I met a man on a plane who was carrying Tom Peters' latest book, *A Passion for Excellence*. I asked how he liked it. He loved it, he said, and then told me that when he had read its predecessor, *In Search of Excellence*, he realized he was working in a company that didn't have any of those earmarks of excellence. He went in search of a place that lived by the tenets Peters and Waterman had written about. He found a small plumbing fixture manufacturer that was a good fit with his values ʳ ᵈ the way in which he wanted to work.

WHEN TO SETTLE FOR LESS

As much as I encourage people to work to find the strongest possible wins for both parties, there are times when it makes sense to compromise. But the problem is that egos can get in the way. Once we begin working toward a goal, it is often difficult to lower our expectations and settle for less. Our urge to win overtakes the reality of the situation. Or sometimes our urge to make sure no one else wins leads to the same behavior. Here are two examples of situations in which it may be better to settle for less:

- **This is all you can get today without harming the relationship.** There are times when you could get more, but you'll lessen the chances of making future agreements. Union and management negotiators are wise to pull back a step and accept a little less than they had hoped for if they believe this gesture will keep the relationship intact.
- **A small win today serves longer-term goals.** Smart salespeople know that a small sale to a happy customer is usually better than a large sale to one who resents you for talking him into buying. While many car salespeople receive a lot of criticism for high-pressure tactics, the better sales people foster amazing loyalty and repeat business.

WHEN TO AVOID THIS BOOK'S ADVICE

It's not likely you made it this far in the book if you don't agree with my ideas. However, just in case, here are two situations when you should avoid trying any of the things I advocate in this book:

- **Your mind is made up and you aren't going to change.** You've decided to take on a new assignment that will benefit the company but will be a strain on those who work closest to you. You know they aren't going to like it in the beginning — or even once they get into it. But you are convinced this assignment is so important that nothing will deter you. You are not open to being influenced. You refuse to consider a watered-down version of the plan or delaying the start by even a month. You don't even want to ask people how they might go about juggling other priorities. You simply want to do it your way. No questions.

When Miles Davis was charting new territory in jazz in the 1960s, many told him this new approach would never work. According to fellow musician Wayne Shorter, Davis would say, "Why don't you get out of the recording studio, get off the stage, stop ringing my doorbell, just shut up and let me do it my way."[3]

If you find yourself in a situation in which you simply cannot be influenced, don't try to apply the principles in this book. They work best in situations in which you care about the outcome and care about the relationship. If you attempt to use these principles when your mind is already made up, you will be using them in bad faith. You'll be better off going ahead with your idea and taking the heat. (You may not be effective, but at least you'll be honest.)

- **You wouldn't concede anything to the other person, even if your life depended on it.** In this situation, you refuse to listen to anything he or she has to say. You see him or her through a Level 3 lens. If you put yourself in a situation in which it only appears as if you want to be influenced, you'll be inviting trouble. These conversations usually make people angry. That not only kills chances of sparking interest in your idea today, but also creates bad blood for the future.

It is important to distinguish among the conditions: Should you play the hand, sit out a round, or leave the game? It's important to look at each new situation with fresh eyes. Make sure that you are seeing things for what they truly are and that you are not relying on old assumptions about the other person.

Taking These Ideas Home

A few clumsy gestures won't make up for ten years of neglect.
— T.V. cartoon character Homer Simpson, in a self-revelation
on the way he treats his wife, Marge

Sal is forty-five years old. She has loyal friends, earns a decent living, and is respected in her field. But the moment she steps off the plane on visits "home" to see her parents, she suddenly becomes twelve years old again. While this may seem like an ideal anti-aging formula, these visits are stressful for everyone. The conflicts that began in adolescence are still alive. Along with keeping her room just as it was, everyone keeps the parent-child relationship just as it was. She returns from these "vacations" more tired than when she left.

Sal is not alone. Something happens to keep issues alive over decades. By this point in your life, you've probably become pretty good at playing your role when you are with your parents. You father says, "So when are you going to get a *real* job?" And you reply, as if on cue, "I *do* have a real job." And the play begins.

AN INVITATION

Over the past few years, as I've used the lenses of understanding, reactions, and trust (and, of course their resistance counterparts) and the principles of engagement, many people have told me how helpful these ideas were in their personal lives.

This final word is an invitation to you to expand the ideas in this book beyond the workplace.

I don't pretend to have any special expertise in working with families. But my intuition and own experiences suggest that these principles have some application at home too. What follows is based in part on my experience and in part on informal conversations with clients about how these ideas apply to relationships at home. With that caveat in mind, please read on.

It might seem that families should be the greatest incubator for reaching the ideal of the I/You relationship. After all, these are people who live together, know one another's good points and bad, see each other through defeat and triumph, share the pain that comes from the illness and death of those close to them. And they are all part of a family that continues generation to generation. Indeed, the intimacy of the family can create strong bonds. Brother to brother and sister to sister intimacy — in which they can share secrets that they would fear saying to anyone else. Couples who take joy in the success of their mates and provide comfort when their partners are troubled. Parents and children who take delight in each other's company.

All these things are possible, but often not realized. This book can't undo a lifetime's practice, nor is it my intent to do so. The things that block close contact with those closest to us are bigger than the scope of this book.

Where the principles in this book might help is in supporting you during those times when you want something and you are committed to meeting your goal in a way that has the potential to strengthen your relationship.

Here are some things that I believe are true, followed by some ideas that may make it a bit easier to move toward I and You.

I AND IT AT HOME

It is easy to create I/It relationships with so-called loved ones. You may wish that Mary Louise was still adorable in her Cinderella tap dance outfit, but the fact that you are about to talk about safe sex with her suggests that she is no longer little and deserves to be met fully. Mary Louise becomes an It when we don't allow her to grow or be different in any way from our ideal.

It can be quite difficult to let go of our image of what we love. We may want children to either remain in some frozen time warp, never changing, or we may see something in them that never was or will be. The doctor parents, who demand their child go to medical school and ignore the fact that she hates science classes but excels at sports, run the risk of treating their daughter as an It. The parents may have had a picture in mind that might have been developed long before this child was born.

Couples do this to each other. In *Please Understand Me*, the authors suggest that some confuse a marriage license with a sculptor's license.[1] Whenever we hold an ideal image of another person, we cannot allow ourselves to see them for who they are. We objectify them. Similar I/It relationship occurs when we hold too tightly to what we think are appropriate roles and behavior. A wife should always . . . A husband should never . . . A child must . . . All suggest that we hold an image of a right way of being and are not able to see something different.

Everything Is Emotional

Just about everything in family dealings is a Level 2 or 3 issue. Very little is just a rational Level 1 issue. Think of your teenage years. Emotions rule what might seem to be the simplest decisions. Something as simple as going to a movie may cause a flood of emotional reactions. Who will be at that show? Who will I be seen with? Will it look bad that I'm not at the party going on right now across town? And finally, way down the list of considerations is the Level 1 question: Do I actually know anything about this movie?

In a teenager, emotional and hormonal responses are occurring within the individual with little outside help. Now add another person to the scenario — someone who makes the simple request to clean my room before I go to the movie. From the parent's vantage point, this seems like a no-brainer. From the adolescent's point of view, this unreasonable request could make me late for the show. If I am late, my friends will leave without me. They'll find someone else to hang out with, I'll be ostracized, a pariah the rest of my days.

This request has Level 2 implications for me as a teenager — from the way I see things, staying to clean my room could have disastrous consequences. And the request probably has Level 3 implications as well. This may not be the first time that my parents and I have argued about this. There is a history. The parent is anticipating what she'll hear and has her rebuttals in mind. I already know what a loser my mom is, and that her purpose in life seems to be to make my life miserable. So, in Groucho Marx's words, "Whatever it is, I'm against it."

Intent Gets Confused

Sometimes a simple request isn't so simple. Imagine the scenario where dad wants to leave his kids with his own parents for the weekend. On the surface this seems like a nice thing to do. A simple transaction. It gives dad a break and allows the grandparents some time with the grandkids.

But dad doesn't like the amount of sugar that his parents give his kids. By the end of a weekend, the kids are buzzing, and it takes hours for them to calm down. No only that, dad believes that too much sugar is bad for their health.

On the surface, dad's intent is fairly simple. He'd like his own parents to feed the kids more nutritious food. But dad's intent is really more complex. He believes that his parents don't approve of the way that he and his partner raise the beloved grandchildren. So now dad wants two things. He wants some boundaries around the raw tonnage of sugar ingested, and he wants his parents' approval. Both may be worthy goals, but they are different.

Trying to play two objectives at the same time doesn't work for actors, for people at work, and certainly not in family relationships. When our intent is unclear, we send odd messages. It sounds like we are talking about diet and the relative merits of the new, improved Gobs O' Chocolate breakfast cereal. But the grandparents hear something in dad's voice that seems out of place with all this talk about food.

This plays out in other adult children to parent relationships as well. Often the parent wants the adult child to change. Or the child wants her parents to change. These requests are seldom said quite that directly. They are often hidden in conversations about almost anything. Which T.V. show to watch while you're together or agreeing on the temperature in the room may seem like simple Level 1 decisions, but lurking beneath is the message "You're doing it wrong. Now change."

Other people have no reason to change who they are just to accommodate us. (It's one of life's unfair rules.) It's better to give up on changing the other person no matter how morally superior we believe we are — and stick to the point. Can we agree on the number of sweet snacks the kids will get? Can we compromise on the temperature in the room? Can I live without "Frasier" tonight?

The Context Is Rich

The advantage of family relationships is that you often know the people and your shared history so well. This information can be very helpful.

Vickie and Cal's eight-year-old daughter plays in a high-level soccer league. Sue is a good athlete, but she is younger than the other girls and so is a tiny bit out of her league. As the decision to try out for the new season approached, Vickie and Cal struggled with conflicting goals. They agreed that Sue's image of herself as a competent athlete was important to maintain; however, they felt that her current team played at a more competitive level than Sue could handle. They thought they knew what was best: Move her to a less competitive team with girls her own age — allowing her to play but putting her in a position to realize more success and less frustration.

They knew that making the decision themselves and just informing their daughter that she was changing teams would be the most efficient way to accomplish this, but they were aware that this was an emotional decision as well as a logistical one. Excluding Sue from the decision-making process would ignore her emotions and make her powerless over decisions that affect her life. (Certainly there are many decisions that eight-year-olds should not have input on, but Vickie and Cal agreed that extracurricular activities were an area where Sue could have some control.)

They asked themselves, "To what extent are we willing to be influenced by Sue?" They agreed that they could be influenced by her if she said, "I really really want to play, and it's important to me to stay on this team." So they were clear about their intention.

Here's where context comes in. They knew from past conversations that Sue would see any statement on her parents' part as a criticism of her skills: "You don't think I'm good enough to play on this team." She would probably react emotionally and feel bad for a couple of days.

They decided that it was important to truly listen to Sue — emotions and all — and to understand that Sue's Level 2 reaction probably wouldn't pass quickly. They knew that, if they allowed time to pass after the emotional part of the conversation, they could then continue the discussion at a more rational level. By separating the exploration phase from the decision phase, they could allow Sue to experience her initial emotions without having to base a decision on them. If any of them tried to make a decision while emotions were so strong, they could make a decision that they all would regret.

Knowing one's self, the other person, and your history together can help you determine how to proceed — and what to avoid. Cal and Vickie's fairly quick preparation allowed them to become clear about their intent and to use their knowledge of the context to prepare themselves so they could listen and explore, rather than try to rush a decision too quickly. (Rushing might have been the result of knee-jerk reactions on everyone's part.)

Development as Context

Children go through developmental stages. Parents tell me they come to expect the terrible two's. It is the time when the child is learning to set limits and play with control. And they assert themselves with no finesse at all. The good thing about this stage is that it is so obvious. It's hard to miss. Other stages of childhood can be somewhat subtler. In attempting to influence, it is important to pay attention to the developmental stage. What worked well with an eleven-year-old could fail miserably two years later.

As you consider the context for engaging a child in a conversation, you might keep in mind that junior is no longer watching "Sesame Street," but is shaving, driving, and doing things on a computer that you can only dream about. Meet him where he is.

At some stages of development, control is more important than at others. It's pretty easy to tell when those stages are in full flower. Just listen to the response you get when you make a request.

Control is important. People, young and old, usually want to feel in control. If your idea threatens their sense of power, they will resist.

Competition

Competition among siblings is not limited to young children. Ask any family attorney about his or her experience handling estate settlements. People who should know better would rather see the family farm go to developers than allow one of their own family members to get too much.

Let's say you are trying to convince your son to do yard work on Saturday. The issue for him might be: "If I agree to mow the lawn, is my sister going to have to do some equally awful job as well? If not, I'm not mowing." These thoughts may not be conscious, but they are real. If you treat the issue as purely Level 1 ("The grass is high; therefore you have to mow it"), you'll probably have a fight. If your intent is to get the yard mowed while keeping some semblance of peace, you may have to find a way to engage him in a way that shows you are sensitive to fairness.

You might wish for competition among sons and daughters to go away, but for now you might take it as a given as you prepare to engage someone else in your family. It is part of the context in many families.

Shifts in Status

If your parents begin to lose their capacity to care for themselves, your relationship with them may change dramatically. The parents' traditional role is to provide care for the child. Even though you may not have needed that type of care for many years, the implicit trust that you could always go home again or count on your parents to help out in a crisis changes. Now they can't take you back and care for you in the same way ever again.

When a parent begins to need help from you, the child, your status is elevated and their status drops. Most people don't talk about this dynamic, but it has a strong impact on your relationship — and consequently on your ability to influence. This shift in status can cause conflict over the simplest issues.

Sometimes these shifts can take comic turns. Take Walter and his mother, for example. Walter is an executive who is used to getting his way. As he saw his mother's strength diminish, he worried that she wore herself out cleaning and cooking for herself. She was independent and demanded that she continue to live alone. He came up with an idea that he felt would help his mom. When he tried to convince her that she should have prepared meals brought in every day, he was surprised at her reaction: "No! Absolutely not." His knee-jerk response: Find a way to make her use a "meals on wheels" service. He hit on what he thought was a brilliant plan. He told her that he had a no-cancellation contract with the service. Even though she didn't like the idea, she was stuck with it.

A couple of weeks later, while visiting his mother, he noticed that no dinner had arrived. When he asked her about this, she told him that they weren't bringing meals anymore. He reminded her that they couldn't cancel the contract. She replied that she called the company, told them she would be on vacation, and would resume the service when she returned.

These issues and their complementary levels of resistance are part of the human experience. Consequently, what you see at work, you see at home. The context and actors may be different, but the issues are similar.

While a knee jerk begets a knee-jerk reaction, the more important point is that we will do things to keep control and to keep the delicate balance of status intact.

Status plays out between parents and younger children as well. While parents may have higher status due to age, role, and resources, children may appreciate and fight against this at the same time. When you want something and your child doesn't, it may have little to do with the Level 1 information — is it a good idea or not? — and a lot more to do with status implications. If the request seems like an order coming from someone who is in a position to demand something from you, either of you may fight or submit and never fully engage with the idea.

Submission may sound attractive, but if your goal is to promote your idea in a way that respects the other person, this can work against what you intend. Submission often results in compliance and not to an enthusiastic commitment to the idea.

Status difference goes with the territory. There are times when a parent may play the "I'm the mommy, that's why!" card, but it is one that can lose its power over time.

When the Relationship Shifts

When status shifts, so does our relationship — sometimes in intense and dramatic ways. Brian's father had become physically very weak. He simply could not take care of himself. For most of his eighty-nine years, his dad had been a fiercely independent man. It was only recently that he had to stop driving, which cut him off from his buddies at his club.

Brian understood this loss but was impatient. He tried to push his father into doing things that were "good for him." His father had little choice since he lacked the physical strength or resources to do anything else, but Brian's actions began to create a rift between them. His father was now forced to play low status in relation to his son's new, more demanding presence. Fortunately, there were other adult children who could temper Brian's insistence.

There is a better way. Gretchen noticed that her mother's mental capacity seemed to be diminishing. She talked with her father about it. He was concerned, but felt that it was just temporary sadness caused by the move into a retirement community.

Her father did take his wife to the family doctor for a checkup. The doctor assured them there was nothing wrong and said that it was the slight memory loss that comes with aging. Nothing to worry about.

Gretchen's mother's condition continued to grow worse. Gretchen suggested that they take her to a major university medical center for tests. Her mother said that she didn't need to go and began blaming the father for scheduling this visit. Gretchen's dad began to have second thoughts. Maybe the family doctor was right. Maybe they should just let things be for a while.

Gretchen was insistent. This exam could be important. She would fly home to attend the screening with her parents. Her intent was to find out what was going on with her mother and find out whether there was anything they could do to help her. As she moved toward this goal and her father pushed back, she had an odd feeling that she was becoming the parent. She was setting boundaries and saying what was important. She was determined not to back off.

She was aware that this was shifting her relationship with her father. She didn't feel she could make a fully collaborative decision since her father was leaning against further testing. He could say no at any time. But Gretchen knew that her dad wanted what was best for his wife of fifty years and that her own strength would serve all of them.

She wanted to make sure that she proceeded in a way that treated her dad with respect. She decided that matching status with him, not playing higher or lower, would be the best course to keep communication open. She told him what she had learned about the university center. She addressed his questions.

She listened to his concerns. He was not a man to talk about feelings and fears, so she tried to listen deeply whenever he gave even a slight objection. She knew this was the only way to stay in contact during these conversations. She did not try to talk him out of his opinions. When he suggested that they wait, she truthfully acknowledged that she wanted to do the same, but was afraid to wait. She asked what he thought of the center. Did he have any other suggestions for ways to proceed? She offered to take the blame. What if she became the one who was pushing for this in her mother's eyes?

Through these conversations, he agreed to go ahead. Gretchen made sure she arrived at her parents' home a couple of days before the appointment. She knew that she and her father probably would not talk about the tests or his feelings, but she wanted to be there to demonstrate that they were in this together.

The tests showed that her mother did have a degenerative brain disorder. Over the coming months and years, Gretchen tried, as best she could, to offer support to her father without making demands. She had to remind herself that this was his wife and that he was fully capable of making decisions regarding care for her.

USING THE PRINCIPLES AT HOME

Many of the ideas that support understanding, favorable reactions, and trust can be adapted and used at home. Here are the major ones I see.

Know Your Own Knee-Jerk Reactions

Members of families can have years of knee-jerk triggers stored on file. Sometimes all a parent has to do is clear his throat and the adult child's knee starts twitching. I urge you to take time to identify the specific triggers. When your mother says, "Why can't you find a nice man to settle down with?" When your father says, "Plastics!" When your sister furrows her brow a certain way. The way your son laughs at you after you explain something important.

Examine these sorts of triggers. What is it about them that bothers you? Here are some of the knee jerks that seem to be triggered in families:

- Attacking your intelligence or questioning your competence
- Attacking your integrity
- Attacking your ideas or beliefs
- Using their status against you
- Threatening your control over your own life

Use this list as a starting point for deeper exploration. If your mother's attack on your values and beliefs is what gets to you, ask yourself why this is so. Perhaps her approval of your values and beliefs is very important to you. Or perhaps there are other reasons. As you identify what triggers the triggers, try to look at your reactions without judgment.

Mindful Reflection

Here is a variation on one of the mindfulness practices covered in chapter 10:

- Pay attention to your breathing. Once you've settled into the rhythm of your breathing, continue to the next step.

- Bring one of the knee-jerk triggers to mind. Allow it to be in your awareness without analyzing or evaluating it. Just let it sit there while you breathe.
- When you are ready, release the thought of the knee-jerk trigger and return your attention to your breathing.

Mindfulness practice does not lend itself to an "I'll use it when I absolutely need to" approach. In other words, you may see limited benefit (if any at all) if you only try to use it the moment your plane touches down on your visit back home. Mindfulness is a discipline, and it requires the same attention as the development of any skill. No musician would wait until the night of a big concert to practice those fingering patterns that gave her so much trouble in earlier performances.

MOVING FORWARD

Applying the principles as a way to encourage understanding, favorable reactions, and sufficient trust to move ahead is challenging. I take some comfort in knowing that if we can improve in these areas while at work, they will transfer to home (as long as we keep our eyes open). And if we learn to apply these principles at home, they can improve our ability to get things accomplished at work.

RESOURCES

Here is a short list of key points, assessments, and tools for quick reference.

The Life or Death of an Idea   *Chapter 1*
Stages of an Idea   page 28
5/5 Test   page 30

Why They Don't Want What You Want   *Chapter 2*
Levels of Resistance
    Level 1   pages 34–36
    Level 2   pages 36–39
    Level 3   pages 39–43
Assessment: Expanding the Frame   page 45
Three Essential Questions   page 46

Know Your Intention   *Chapter 4*
Martin Buber's I/You   pages 64–65
Guidelines for Creating a Clear Intention   pages 69–75
    Focus on Issues + Focus Long Term + Focus on the
    Relationship + Focus on What Can Be Observed
Act "As If"   page 73
Mantra   page 77

Consider the Context   *Chapter 5*
Reactions to the Idea (Level 2)   pages 83–85
    History of the Idea + Your Idea in Conflict with
    Their Idea + Idea Is a Threat + Word on the Street +
    Resilience versus Burnout + Other Bad Timing Issues
Trust Issues (Level 3)   pages 85–91
    Your History Together + What You Represent +
    Relative Rank and Status + Effect of Environment
    on Your Relationship + Impact of Beliefs
Assessment: Exploring My Beliefs   page 92

Avoid Knee-Jerk Reactions
What Hooks Us
Types of Knee-Jerk Reactions
Avoiding Knee-Jerk Reactions
    Focus on Intent + Know Your Triggers + Practice
    + Use a "Mouth Brace" + Wait for a Better Time
Ways to Stop Mid-Jerk
    Catch Yourself + Shift Attention + Shift to I/You +
    Take a Break + Admit What's Happening to You
Assessment: Stop Mid-Jerk

Chapter 6
pages 95–96
pages 97–99
pages 103–105

pages 105–108

page 107

Pay Attention
Ways to Pay Attention
    Listen to Be Changed + Leaning In and Leaning Away
    + Act in the Moment
Signals You're Not Paying Attention in the Moment
Paying Attention after the Conversation
Becoming More Adept at Paying Attention

Chapter 7
pages 112–117

page 115
pages 117–118
pages 118–121

Explore Deeply
What It Takes to Explore Effectively
    Shut Up and Listen + Put Your Goals Aside
    Temporarily + Be Willing to Be Influenced by What
    You Hear + Go Deeper than You'd Probably Like +
    Be Willing to Seek Common Ground
Coffee with Joe
Develop Worst-Case Scenarios
Ways to Explore Deeply
    Find a Safe Way to Talk + Listen to Grok +
    Put Skin in the Game + Put Limits on the Work +
    Respect the Other Person's Distance
Knowing When You've Explored Enough

Chapter 8
pages 126–130

page 127
page 129
pages 131–135

pages 135–136

Find Ways to Connect
A Process for Connecting
Embrace the Paradox
    A Template + Pre-existing Conditions
Other Ways to Connect
    The Believing Game + Trial Balloon Proposal +
    Win-Win Lite

Chapter 9
pages 140–141

pages 141–143
pages 144–146

Stay Calm to Stay Engaged
Mindfulness Skills
    Relaxation Response + Lost Art of Breathing +
    Counting Your Breaths + Graduate-Level Breathing +
    Focus on Your Center of Gravity

Chapter 10
pages 155–158

Other Ways to Prepare   pages 158–164
    Rehearse to Break Bad Habits + Find Your
    Achilles' Heel + Use a Coach + Debriefing + Support
    Yourself during the Exchange + Let Go of What You
    Know + Put Things in Perspective
Mindfulness in the Moment   pages 164–167
    A Game Plan + Breathing + Three-Point Check +
    Take a Break

Ways to Avoid Resistance in the First Place   *Chapter 11*
Transactions versus Connections   pages 170–173
Ideas for Building Stronger Relationships   page 172
Repairing Level 3 Relationships   pages 177–182
    Firm Belief in I and You + Make the First Move +
    Find Common Concerns + Keep Commitments +
    Mea Culpa + Forgive Them + Turn Your Cards Face Up +
    Find Opportunities to Listen
Assessment: How You Can Tell Relationships Are Working   pages 179–180

What to Do When the Principles Aren't Enough   *Chapter 12*
When to Apply the Principles   pages 188
When to Wait   pages 188–189
When to Leave   pages 189–192
When to Settle for Less   pages 192
When to Avoid This Book's Advice   pages 192–193

A Final Word: Taking These Ideas Home
At Home   pages 196–204
    Everything is Emotional + Intent Gets Confused +
    Context Is Rich + Shifts in Status + Shifts in
    Relationships
Using the Principles at Home   pages 205–206
    Know Your Own Knee-Jerk Reactions +
    Mindful Reflection

OTHER RESOURCES

www.beyondresistance.com

Please visit my Website www.beyondresistance.com for additional resources. You'll find a current list of books, articles, Website links, and other resources that I recommend ... Assessment tools and articles you can print and copy at no charge ... Frequently asked questions ... And perhaps, most important, an opportunity to engage in conversation with other readers about the issues covered in this book.

ENDNOTES

Chapter 2: Why They Don't Want What You Want
1. Roger Penrose, review of *Fermat's Enigma*, by Simon Singh, *New York Times Book Review*, November 30, 1997, 12.
2. Bryan Miller, "The Wizard of Pop Who Turned on the Guitar," *New York Times*, June 4, 1995, p. 26, col. 1.
3. Jonathan Clements, "Getting Going," *The Wall Street Journal*, June 23, 1998, C1.
4. Joseph LeDoux, *The Emotional Brain* (New York: Simon & Schuster, 1996).
5. Charles Darwin, *The Expression of Emotions in Man and Animals* (Chicago: University of Chicago Press, 1965).
6. LeDoux, *Emotional Brain*, 131.
7. Curt Suplee, "Stressed Women Turn to Mother Nature, Study Says," *The Washington Post*, May 19, 2000, A2.
8. John Gottman, *What Predicts Divorce* (Hillsdale, N.J.: Lawrence Erlbaum Associates, 1994).
9. Steven Pinker, *How the Mind Works* (New York: Norton, 1997), 345.
10. Gottman, *What Predicts Divorce*.
11. John Lewis, op-ed piece in remembrance of George Wallace, *New York Times*, September 16, 1998.
12. LeDoux, *Emotional Brain*, 53.

Chapter 3: The Art of Building Commitment
1. Felix Grant, quoted in Ken Ringle's "Felix Grant, for the Love of Jazz," *The Washington Post*, November 12, 1989.
2. Interview with Jack Lemmon, "Inside the Actors Studio," Bravo Network, 1999.
3. Told to me by British theater director Keith Johnstone.

Chapter 4: Know Your Intention
1. Uri Savir, *The Process* (New York: Vintage, 1998), 14–15.
2. Martin Buber, *I and Thou*, translated by Walter Kaufman (New York: Touchstone, 1996). Buber's *Ich und Du* is commonly translated as I and Thou. However, You is also an acceptable translation, and one that I

believe is more appropriate to the spirit of this book. While Buber focuses on relationships between people, he also extends Thou to one's relationship with his or her God. My intent with this book is to limit the focus to people relating to other people, therefore You seems a better translation.

3. Eleni Chamis, "Bethesda Lawyer Encourages Logic Not Litigation," *Washington Business Journal*, February 4–10, 2000.
4. Roger Fisher and William Ury, *Getting to Yes* (New York: Penguin, 1981), 4.
5. Ron Shapiro et al., *The Power of Nice* (New York: John Wiley & Sons, 1998).
6. Pinker, *How the Mind Works*, 373.
7. Ulric Neisser, *Cognition and Reality* (San Francisco: Freeman, 1976).

Chapter 5: Consider the Context

1. Patti Waldmeir, *Anatomy of a Miracle* (New York: W.W. Norton, 1997), 61.
2. Nelson Mandela, *Long Walk to Freedom* (Boston: Little Brown & Co., 1995).
3. Ibid.
4. Eliot Aronson, *The Social Animal* (New York: W. H. Freeman, 1985).
5. Neil Rackham, *SPIN Selling* (New York, McGraw-Hill, 1998).
6. Daryl Conner, *Managing at the Speed of Change* (New York: Villard, 1993). Conner says that a sponge can only hold so much liquid and suggests that we need to find ways to increase the size of the sponge if we want to increase people's resilience.
7. Terry Anderson, *Den of Lions* (New York: Crown, 1993), 118–119.
8. Aronson, *Social Animal*, 88.
9. Keith Johnstone, *Impro for Storytellers* (New York: Routledge, 1999), 221.
10. Philip Zimbardo, "The Psychological Power and Pathology of Imprisonment." Statement prepared for a U.S. House of Representatives committee on prison reform, October 25, 1971. Journalist Ted Conover's *Newjack* (New York: Vintage, 2001) provides an interesting variation on this theme. Conover took a job as a guard at Sing Sing and saw shifts occur in his relationships at work and at home.
11. Arthur Jones, as quoted in David P. Hanna, *Designing Organizations for High Performance* (Reading, Mass.: Addison-Wesley, 1988), 38.

Chapter 6: Avoid Knee-Jerk Reactions

1. George J. Mitchell, *Making Peace* (New York: Knopf, 1999), 52–53.
2. LeDoux, *Emotional Brain*, 17.
3. Ibid.
4. Ibid.

5. Robert Cialdine, *Influence* (New York: Quill, 1984), 254–255. Wood's quote came from B. MacKenzie's article, "When Sober Executives Went on a Bidding Binge," *TV Guide*, June 22, 1974.

6. C. George Boeree, *Personality Theories: Biography of Karen Horney*, www.ship.edu/~cgboerre/horney.html. Many have explored similar terrain. Edwin Nevis and Richard Wallen credit Horney in their work (paper from the Gestalt Institute of Cleveland). Elias Porter credits Eric Fromm with his model of personal strengths.

7. 1992 interview by Terry Gross with Tom Blanton, "Fresh Air," National Public Radio, rebroadcast January 12, 2001.

8. David Halberstam, *The Children* (New York: Fawcett Books, 1998).

9. LeDoux, *Emotional Brain*, 53.

10. Keith Johnstone, conversation, July 2000.

11. Interview with Robert Dwan, author of *As Long as They're Laughing: Groucho Marx and You Bet Your Life*, "Morning Edition," National Public Radio, April 4, 2001.

Chapter 7: Pay Attention

1. Anderson, *Den of Lions*, 318–319.

2. Tom Peters and Robert Waterman, *In Search of Excellence* (New York: Harper & Row, 1982), 56–57.

3. Daniel Goleman, *Fortune*, October 26, 1998, 294.

4. Carl Rogers, *On Becoming a Person* (Boston: Houghton Mifflin, 1972).

5. "Dialogue Between Wallace Shawn and Andre Gregory," *New York Times*, May 16, 1999, AR5.

6. Alan Alda, "Inside the Actors Studio," Bravo Network, 2000.

7. Claudia Koonz, review of *Albert Speer: His Battle with Truth*, by Gitta Sereny, *New York Times Book Review*, October 8, 1995.

8. W. Timothy Gallwey, *The Inner Game of Tennis* (New York: Random House, 1997).

9. Arnold Beisser, "The Paradoxical Theory of Change" (www.gestalt.org/arnie.htm). A classic article (1970) that suggests change occurs when we are fully aware of the current state. This paper goes beyond learning and suggests that most change occurs when we heighten awareness and fully embrace the current conditions.

10. Pinker, *How the Mind Works*, 366.

11. Neil Rackham, personal conversation, May 24, 2001.

12. Pinker, *How the Mind Works*, 415.

Chapter 8: Explore Deeply

1. Stephanie Gruner, "How Can I Get Employees to Buy In to Our Strategy?" *Inc.*, October 1997, 113.

2. LeDoux, *Emotional Brain*, 17.

3. "Ally McBeal," Fox Television Network, April 13, 1998.

4. Stephen Covey, *The 7 Habits of Highly Effective People* (New York: Simon and Schuster, 1989), 237.
5. David Halberstam, *The Best and the Brightest* (New York: Random House, 1969).
6. Robert Grudin, *On Dialogue* (New York: Houghton Mifflin, 1996).
7. Dante, *The Inferno*, translated by John Ciardi (New York: New American Library, 1993).
8. Mitchell, *Making Peace*, 156.
9. Rick Maurer, "Interview with Peter Johnson," *Beyond the Wall of Resistance* (Austin, Tex.: Bard Books, 1996), 145–147.
10. Anne Glauber, "If You're at War with Your Teenager, Try E-mail," *USA Today*, May 20, 1997, 13A.
11. Robert Heinlein, *Stranger in a Strange Land* (New York: Putnam, 1961).
12. Neil Rackham, personal conversation, May 24, 2001.

Chapter 9: Find Ways to Connect

1. Roberta Maynard, "A Creative Alternative to Downsizing: Rhino Foods 'Loans' Employees to Other Companies Instead of Laying Them Off," *Nation's Business*, January 1, 1994.
2. Ted Castle, "A Creative Way to Avoid Layoffs," *Nation's Business*, August 1, 1997, 6.
3. Barry Johnson, *Polarity Management* (Amherst, Mass.: Human Resources Development Press, 1997).
4. Peter Elbow, *Embracing Contraries* (New York: Oxford University Press, 1986), 257.
5. Guy Kawasaki, *Rules for Revolutionaries* (New York: HarperBusiness, 1999).
6. "Shoptalk," interview with Jason Ward and David Garrett, *New York Times Magazine*, November 12, 2000.

Chapter 10: Stay Calm to Stay Engaged

Opening epigraph from Peter Brook, *Threads of Time* (Washington, D.C.: Counterpoint, 1998), 61.
1. Gallwey, *Inner Game of Tennis*, 22.
2. Herbert Benson, *The Relaxation Response* (New York: Harper Torch, 2000).
3. Tara Bennett-Goleman, *Emotional Alchemy* (New York: Random House/Harmony, 2001), 9.
4. Keith Johnstone, *Impro: Improvisation and the Theatre* (New York: Routledge, 1981).
5. I learned this technique from courses at the now defunct Mid-Atlantic Association for Training and Consulting. I have no idea where this simple model originated.
6. *The Paleface*, Universal Studios, 1948.

7. Interview with Laura Linney and Mark Ruffalo, "The Charlie Rose Show," Canadian Broadcasting Corporation, December 8, 2000.
8. Madeline Bruser, *The Art of Practicing* (New York: Bell Tower, 1997), 61.

Chapter 11: Ways to Avoid Resistance in the First Place
1. "Interview with Marietta Jaeger," *These Times*, March 22, 1998, 5.
2. Rick Maurer, "Interview with Peter Johnson," *Beyond the Wall of Resistance* (Austin, Tex.: Bard Books, 1996), 145–147.

Chapter 12: What to Do When the Principles Aren't Enough
1. This chapter is adapted from a segment in my book *Building Capacity for Change Sourcebook* (Arlington, Va.: Maurer & Associates, 2000).
2. A reader of the first draft urged me to remove this example since going to topless clubs with staff is illegal and therefore the example was trite. Sadly, the story is true.
3. Geoffrey Himes, "Hancock and Shorter: Daring Duo," *Washington Post Weekend*, August 15, 1997, 11.

A Final Word: Taking These Ideas Home
1. David Kiersey and Marilyn Bates, *Please Understand Me* (Del Mar, Calif.: Prometheus Nemesis Books, 1984).

ACKNOWLEDGMENTS

Thanks to the many people who contributed to this book. In addition to those I name here, there are many others whose examples of trying to influence with integrity inspired me. In many cases these are people I don't even know, but I saw them engage and work with others in airports and offices and restaurants. Seeing these people over the years gave me hope that we can get what we want in ways that respect others.

I truly appreciate the thoughtful critique of my ideas and of various drafts of this book from JoAnn Barton, Frederick Bryant, John Carter, Patti Danos, Mike Hopp, Diane Johnson, Danielle Johnston, Phil Kalin, Matt Kayhoe, Cindy Kazan, Mark LeBlanc, Janet Long, LeRoy Pingho, Peter Postorino, Marian Reiss, Diane Russ, Susan Schroeer, Rick Seikely, Max Stark, Mike Walsh, and Marc Young. These people forced me to look more closely at what I was trying to say. I believe this is a better book because of your candid comments.

When I described the book I was thinking about writing, my friend Anne Anderson said, "Here's an idea for a title: Why don't you want what I want?" We played with many other more corporate-sounding (and boring) titles, but kept coming back to this one. Thank you so much.

Gestalt psychology gave me a way to begin to look at these issues. While my work deviates somewhat from that thinking, anyone familiar with Gestalt theory and practice will recognize the influence it has had on my work. I owe special thanks to the faculty of the Gestalt Therapy Institute of the Pacific and to my colleagues at the Gestalt Institute of Cleveland, where I teach in the Organization and Systems Development Program.

A special thanks to my friend and business partner at Maurer & Associates, Sandy Honour, who supports, critiques, and makes space for me to write.

Thanks to my editor, Leslie Stephen, who has helped me shape this book and turn ideas into chapters. And to Ray Bard, publisher of Bard Press, for his continued confidence in my work. One of the joys of the writing process was getting to work with both of you again. Thank you to Deborah Costenbader for your attention to detail and style.

And thanks to my wife, Kathy. Your encouragement helped me stick with this book, but that doesn't begin to embrace the deep support I feel from you that allows me to explore all manner of sacred, profane, and mundane activities.

ABOUT THE AUTHOR

Rick Maurer is an advisor to individuals and organizations on ways to build support for change. He is the author of *Beyond the Wall of Resistance*, as well as three other books and many articles on leadership and change. He works with a wide range of clients, from high-tech to government to finance to healthcare, in North America, South America, and Europe. His opinions have been sought by *Fortune*, *The Economist*, *The Wall Street Journal*, *NBC Nightly News*, and CNBC. In addition to having the usual fairly boring academic credentials, he has worked in theater as a writer and director, was a professional musician, and is an aging kayaker.

Maurer & Associates
Through consulting, speaking, and seminars, Maurer & Associates works with individuals and organizations to help them accelerate implementation of change in ways that build commitment. For a complete description of their services, visit www.beyondresistance.com. You can also access additional tools related to *Why Don't You Want What I Want?* from this Website.

INDEX

Abortion, 130, 178
Acheson, Dean, 102
Acting in the moment, 115–17
Active listening, 110–11. *See also*
 Listening
Actors, 53, 57, 73, 75, 77, 112,
 121–22, 159, 163. *See also*
 Theater improvisation
Adolescents, 132, 134, 197–98
AFL-CIO, 178
Africa, 79–80, 181
Aikido, 101, 153
Airlines, 55–57, 75–77
Ala, Abu, 63–64, 68, 74
Alda, Alan, 112, 121–22, 132
"Ally McBeal," 126
Amygdala, 38, 95
Anatomy of a Miracle
 (Waldmeir), 79
Anderson, Terry, 86, 109
Anxiety reactions, 97–99
Aronson, Eliot, 80–81
Art of War (Sun Tzu), 70
"As if" tactic, 73
Attention. *See* Paying attention
Awareness. *See* Paying attention

Bad timing issues, 85, 104, 188–89
Banks, 24, 27, 29, 31, 173–74
Beckett, Samuel, 153
Beemer, Bob, 85
Beisser, Arnold, 212 (ch7,n9)
Beliefs
 attack on, 96
 questions on, 91, 92
 relationships and, 90–91,
 173–75
 self-assessment on, 92
Believing Game versus Doubting
 Game, 144–45

Benson, Herbert, 155
Berlin Stories (Isherwood), 145
Berra, Yogi, 78
Beyond the Wall of Resistance
 (Maurer), 14
Bierce, Ambrose, 93
Blanton, Tom, 102
Block, Peter, 53–54
Body language, 97–98, 113–15,
 119, 120
Brain research, 35, 38, 75
Breaks, 106–107, 166–67
Breathing, 104, 156–57, 165, 205
Brighton Beach Memoirs
 (Simon), 117
Broderick, Matthew, 117
Buber, Martin, 14, 64, 211 (ch4,n2)
Burnout, 84–85, 189
Burr, Aaron, 96

Cabaret, 145
Castle, Ted, 142–43
Cat Ballou, 91
Center of gravity, 157–58
Change. *See also* Engagement
 principles; Resistance
 awareness and, 212 (ch7,n9)
 listening and, 112–13
 and one-to-one relationships
 generally, 13–15
 questions on, 11–13
 refusal to, 192–93
 and resilience versus burnout,
 84–85, 189
Chenier, Phil, 67
Chicago, 144
Children. *See* Family relationships;
 Parent-child relationship
Civil Rights movement, 41, 103
Clausewitz, Carl von, 70

Coaching, 160–62
Commitment
 avoidance of knee-jerk reactions, 51–52, 56, 93–108
 and connection with others'
 goals, 54, 56, 139–49
 context and, 50–51, 56, 79–92
 example on building, 47–48
 and exploration of others'
 reactions, 53–54, 56,
 123–38
 intention and, 49–50, 56, 63–78
 mastery of, 57
 paying attention and, 52–53,
 56, 109–22
 principles of engagement for
 building, 49–57
 trust and keeping commitments, 178, 181
Common concerns, 130, 178
Common Ground Network for
 Life and Choice, 130
Communication. *See also*
 Engagement principles;
 Listening; Relationships
 barrier to, 110–11
 fear response and, 37–38,
 43–46, 54, 125
 finding safe way to talk, 131–32
 humor in, 120
 I/It relationship and, 64,
 65–69, 70
 I/You relationship and, 64–65,
 67–78, 102, 131–32
 and leaning in and leaning
 away movements,
 113–15, 119
 missed signals and, 109–10
 non-verbal communication,
 97–98, 113–15, 119, 120

parent-teen communication,
132, 134, 197–98

paying attention to style of,
120–21

shift from I/It to I/You relationship, 68–77, 106–107,
111–12

status differences and, 88

talking-listening balance in,
120

understanding and, 127–28

and willingness to be influenced, 128, 143

Compliance, malicious, 118

Conflict between ideas, 83–84

Connection with others' goals

Believing Game versus
Doubting Game, 144–45

continuous connection,
146–47

embracing paradox of, 141–43

pre-existing conditions
for, 143

as principle of engagement,
54, 56, 139–49

process for, 140–41

Rackham on sales, 147–49

reactions and, 145

trial balloon proposal, 145

trust and, 145

understanding and, 145

and willingness to be
influenced, 143

win-win and, 146

Conner, Daryl, 84–85, 211 (ch5,n6)

Conover, Ted, 211 (ch5,n10)

Consultants, 29–30

Context

and bad timing issues, 85

beliefs and relationships,
90–91, 92

and conflict between ideas,
83–84

elements of, 82–91

environment and relation-
ships, 88–90

of family relationships,
199–201

group representation and
trust, 41–42, 86, 190

and history of the idea, 83

history together and trust, 86

and idea as threat, 84

paying attention to, 91

as principle of engagement,
50–51, 56, 79–92

and reactions to ideas, 82–85

ative rank and status, 87–88

resilience versus burnout,
84–85, 189

sales and, 81–82

significance of, 80–81

trust and, 85–91

Control issues, 200–201

Conversation versus presentation,
34, 43–44

Covey, Stephen, 127, 129

Crisp, Quentin, 187

Cuban Missile Crisis, 102

Cultural background, 42

Customer service, 89, 111–12, 131

Danger. *See* Fear response

Dante, 57, 129, 130, 134, 183

Darwin, Charles, 36, 38

Davis, Miles, 193

Defensiveness, 56, 111, 125–26

Differences. *See* Exploration of
others' reactions

Diller, Barry, 96

Distrust. *See* Trust

Divorce, 70–71

Doubting Game versus Believing
Game, 144–45

Ebb, Fred, 144–45

Einstein versus Neanderthal
reaction, 38–39

Elbow, Peter, 144

Emotional Intelligence
(Goleman), 110

Emotions, 120, 137–38, 197–98.
See also Fear response;
Reactions

Engagement principles. *See also*
Reactions; Trust;
Understanding

avoidance of knee-jerk reactions, 51–52, 56, 93–108

burnout and, 84–85, 189

calm and alert readiness for
engagement, 153–67

clear intention, 49–50, 56,
63–78

connection with others' goals,
54, 56, 139–49

context, 50–51, 56, 79–92

examples of, 55–57

exploration of others' reactions, 53–54, 56, 123–38

for family relationships,
195–206

leave versus stay decision,
189–92

mastery of, 57

mindfulness skills and, 155–67

overextension and, 189

paying attention, 52–53, 56,
109–22

preparation for meeting the
other person, 154

situations for applying, 188

situations for avoiding this
book's advice, 192–93

situations for leaving, 189–92

situations for settling for
less, 192

situations for waiting, 188–89

timing issues for, 85, 104,
188–89

Environment. *See also* Context

questions on, 89

relationships and, 88–90

Escalation, 102

Excitement, 176–77. *See also*
Engagement

Exploration of others' reactions

and acceptance of blame, 130

challenge and hope of, 131

deep exploration, 128–30

defensiveness and, 125–26

difficulties of, 124–26

and fear of the unknown, 126

fear response and, 125, 129

and finding safe way to talk,
131–32

honest responses to others'
reactions, 133–34

humor and, 130

and I/You relationship, 131–32

Jacobs on, 136–38

and knee-jerk reactions, 128

knowing when to stop, 135–36

listening and, 53–54, 127,
132–33

and need for speed, 125

planning and, 129

as principle of engagement,
53–54, 56, 123–38

and putting aside own goal
temporarily, 127–28

putting limits on, 134

reasons for exploring differences, 123–24
and respect for other's dis-
tance, 134–35
and seeking common
ground, 130
techniques for effective
approach to, 126–30
techniques for exploring
deeply, 131–35
trust and, 133
understanding and,
127–30, 133
and willingness to be influenced, 128
worst-case scenarios and, 129

Family relationships
child development and,
200–201
context of, 199–201
control issues and, 200–201
couple relationships, 40–41, 197
distrust within marriage,
40–41
divorce and, 70–71
emotions in, 197–98
engagement principles for,
195–206
as I/It relationships, 196–204
intention in, 198–99
knee-jerk reactions and,
202, 205
mindfulness skills and,
205–206
parent-child relationship, 132,
134, 164, 171, 177–78, 195,
196–204
shifts in, 203–204
sibling competition and, 201
status shifts and, 201–203
teenagers and, 132, 134,
197–98
Fear of the unknown, 126
Fear response, 36–39, 43–46, 54,
84, 94–95, 106, 125, 129,
139, 164
Federalist Papers (Hamilton), 96
Feedback sessions, 174
Fermat's Theorem, 34
Fight or flight reaction, 36–39,
44–46, 94–95
Fisher, Roger, 69, 71–72
5/5 test, 30

Forgiveness, 41, 108, 181,
183–85
Fromm, Erich, 212 (ch6,n6)
Frozen state, 99
Funny Lady, 144

Gallwey, Timothy, 118–19, 154
Garrett, David, 146
Gender differences
in relationships, 174
in stress management, 37
Genet, Jean, 79
Gestalt Therapy Institute, 136
Getting to Yes (Fisher and Ury),
69, 71
Glauber, Anne, 132, 134
Goals
brain research on, 75
connection with others' goals
as engagement principle,
54, 56, 139–49
intention and, 74–75
setting aside own goal, 127–28
and small wins, 192
Goetzmann, William, 35
Goleman, Daniel, 110
Gottmann, John, 37–38, 40
Grant, Felix, 51
Gregory, Andre, 112
Grok, 132
Groups
attack on, 96
representation of, 41–42,
86, 190
Grudin, Robert, 128

Hamilton, Alexander, 96
Hanna, David, 89
Hansberry, Lorraine, 19
Harley Davidson Company, 123
Harriman, Averell, 128
Harvard University, 155
Heinlein, Robert, 132
History together and trust,
40–41, 86
Hitler, Adolf, 117
Hoffer, Eric, 63
"Honeymooners," 41
Hope, Bob, 163
Horney, Karen, 97, 101, 212
(ch6,n6)
Hospitals, 23–24, 26, 29, 31, 84,
139–41
Hostage situation, 86, 109

I/It relationship, 64, 65–69, 70,
108, 174, 177, 196–204
I/You relationship
and engagement principles
generally, 188
and exploring differences,
131–32
ideas and, 64–65, 67–69
intention and, 64–65, 67–78
interrupting I/You contact, 102
knee-jerk reactions and,
106–107, 108
lack of belief in, 174
paying attention and, 111–12
and relationship-based
exchanges, 176
and repairing relationships of
mistrust, 177
shift from I/It to, 68–77,
106–107, 108, 111–12
translation of *Ich und Du* as,
211 (ch4,n2)
trust and, 177, 182
I/you relationship, 97–98, 102
i/YOU relationship, 98, 102
i/you relationship, 98–99, 102
IAG (identify, analyze, and generalize) technique, 162
Ideas
active opposition to, 27
attack on, 95
in bank, 24, 27, 29, 31
championing of, 26–27
conflict between, 83–84
dragging feet over, 27
examples of, 23–25
failure in implementation of,
19–20
5/5 test on support for, 30
and getting too far ahead of
others, 21–22
going along with, 27
history of, 83
in hospitals, 23–24, 26, 29, 31,
84, 139–41
I/It relationship and, 64, 65–69
I/You relationship and, 64–65,
67–69
ignoring of, 96
implementation of, 19–31
lack of trust and, 33–34,
39–46
lack of understanding of,
33–36, 45, 46

limited view of, 20–23
missing others' reactions to,
  22–23
negative emotional reactions
  to, 33–34, 36–39, 43–46
reactions to, 26–27, 29, 31, 45
in school system, 24–25, 26, 31
stages of, 38
successful implementation of,
  23–31
support for, 27
as threat, 36–39, 43–46, 54, 84
trust and, 29–31, 45
understanding and, 25–26,
  31, 45
Ignoring
  of opposition, 97
  of others and ideas, 96
Impact, lessening of, 98
Implementation of ideas. *See* Ideas
Impro (Johnstone), 77, 159
Improvisation work, 75, 77, 88,
  115–16. *See also* Actors
In Search of Excellence (Peters
  and Waterman), 172, 191
Influence. *See also* Engagement
  principles; Relationships
  connection and willingness to
    be influenced, 143
  exploring differences and
    willingness to be influ-
    enced, 128
  listening and willingness to be
    changed, 112–13, 132
  and one-to-one relationships
    generally, 13–15, 171
  push versus pull styles of, 149
  questions on, 11–13
  refusal to be influenced,
    192–93
Information, 84, 181–82
Intelligence, attack on, 95
Intention
  "as if" tactic and, 73
  and avoidance of knee-jerk
    reactions, 103
  clarification of, on the fly,
    75–77
  clear intention as principle of
    engagement, 49–50, 56,
    63–78
  confusion of, in family rela-
    tionships, 198–99

goals and, 74–75
guidelines on, 69, 71–75
I/It relationship, 64, 65–69, 70
I/You relationship, 64–65,
  67–78, 188
issues versus positions, 69,
  71–72
long-term focus and, 72–74
mantras and, 77
of paying attention, 110–11
politics and, 70–71
relationship focus and, 74
shift from I/It to I/You relationship, 68–77, 106–107,
  111–12
watching versus paying attention, 77–78
Interests versus positions, 69,
  71–72
Investing, 35, 51–52
Ireland, 58–60, 93–94
Isherwood, Christopher, 144–45
Israel, 63–64, 68, 74
Issues versus positions, 69, 71–72

Jacobs, Lynne, 136–38
Jaeger, Marietta, 181
Jazz, 51, 193
Johnson, Barry, 143
Johnson, Peter, 182
Johnstone, Keith, 77, 88, 106, 159

Kander, John, 144–45
Kawasaki, Guy, 146
Khrushchev, Nikita, 128
Kiss of the Spider Woman, 144
Knee-jerk reactions. *See also*
  Reactions
  and admitting what's happen-
    ing, 107–108
  avoidance of, as principle of
    engagement, 51–52, 56,
    103–105, 164
  awareness versus, 99
  and bad timing issues, 104
  causes of, 94–95
  consequences of, 99, 101–103
  distrust and, 100–101, 103
  escalation and, 102
  and exploration of
    differences, 128
  family relationships and,
    202, 205

to fear, 44–46, 94–95, 139
focus on intent for avoidance
  of, 103
frozen state, 99
and interrupting I/You contact, 102
moving against, 97–98, 101
moving away, 98–99, 101
moving toward, 98, 101
physical reactions and, 105
practice for avoidance of, 104
questions on, 107, 108
relaxation for avoidance of, 104
relaxed concentration for
  identifying, 119
and shift to I/You relationship,
  106–107, 108
signals of, 105–106, 108,
  119, 159
and stopping in midjerk,
  105–108
and taking a break, 106–107
triggers for, 95–96, 103–104,
  205, 206
types of, 97–99
Kurasawa, Akira, 153

Lack of trust. *See* Trust
Lack of understanding. *See*
  Understanding
Lasater, Nancy, 69, 72
Lawson, James, 103
Lawton, Jennifer, 123
Leaning in and leaning away
  movements, 113–15, 119
Leave versus stay decision,
  189–92
Lebanon hostage situation, 86, 109
LeDoux, Joseph, 36, 38
Legal system, 69, 70–71, 72,
  87–88
Lemmon, Jack, 53
Lewis, John, 41
Linney, Laura, 163
Listening. *See also* Exploration
  of others' reactions;
  Paying attention
  active listening, 110–11
  Alda on, 112, 121–22, 132
  in conversation versus presen-
    tation, 43
  and exploring differences,
    53–54, 127–28, 132–33

intention and, 50
paying attention and, 55, 56, 110–13
in relational therapy, 136–38
Rogers on responsive listening, 132–33
talking-listening balance in conversations, 120
trust and, 182
and willingness to be changed, 112–13, 132
Litigation. *See* Legal system
Long-term focus, 72–74

"M.A.S.H.," 121
Machiavelli, Niccolò, 70
Major Account Sales Strategy (Rackham), 147
Making Peace (Mitchell), 58–60
Malicious compliance, 118
Management by wandering around, 172
Managing at the Speed of Change (Conner), 84–85, 211 (ch5,n6)
Mandela, Nelson, 79–80, 81
Mantras, 77
Marriage. *See* Family relationships
Martial arts, 101, 153, 157
Marvin, Lee, 91
Marx, Groucho, 107, 198
Matthau, Walter, 53, 57
McGraw, Bryan, 47–48
Mea culpa, 181
Meetings
paying attention in, 53, 116–17
staff meetings, 172
Mid-Atlantic Association for Training and Consulting, 213 (ch10,n5)
Middle East, 63–64, 68, 74
Mindfulness skills
application of, 167
breathing exercises, 156–57, 165, 205
coach's role in, 160–62
debriefing oneself, 162
family relationships and, 205–206
focus on center of gravity, 157–58
game plan for, 165

IAG (identify, analyze, and generalize) technique, 162
identifying own fears, 159–60
paying attention to own physical reactions, 164–66
rehearsing to break habitual responses, 158–59
relaxation response, 155–56
support for yourself during exchange, 162–64
taking breaks, 166–67
Mistrust. *See* Trust
Mitchell, George, 58–60, 93–94
"Mouth brace" analogy, 104
Movies, 91, 144–45, 146, 153, 163
Moving against, 97–98, 101
Moving away, 98–99, 101
Moving toward, 98, 101
Murder Victims' Families for Reconciliation, 181
Music, 35, 51, 193

Nazi Germany, 117, 190
Neanderthal versus Einstein reaction, 38–39
Neanderthal versus Neanderthal reaction, 44–46
Negative emotional reactions, 33–34, 36–39, 43–46
Nelson, Mariah Burton, 183–85
NET Daemons Associates, 123
Nevis, Edwin, 212 (ch6,n6)
New York, New York, 144
Newjack (Conover), 211 (ch5,n10)
Non-verbal communication, 97–98, 113–15, 119, 120
Northern Ireland, 58–60, 93–94

Office politics, 70–71
On Dialogue (Grudin), 128
On War (Clausewitz), 70
O'Neill, Tip, 31
Open book management, 181–82
Opposition to ideas, 27, 97

Paisley, Ian, 58, 93
Paradox, 141–43
Parent-child relationship, 132, 134, 164, 171, 177–78, 195, 196–204. *See also* Family relationships
Passion for Excellence (Peters), 191

Paul, Les, 35
Paying attention. *See also* Listening
and acting in the moment, 115–17
Alda on, 112, 121–22, 132
to audience during presentations, 111, 114–15
to context, 91
after conversation, 117–18
to emotions, 120
to exploring differences, 136
improvement strategies for, 118–21
intention at key to, 110–11
to leaning in and leaning away movements of others, 113–15, 119
and listening to be changed, 112–13
in meetings, 53, 116–17
missed signals and, 109–10
to physical reactions, 105, 164–66
as principle of engagement, 52–53, 56, 109–22
to reactions of self and others, 52–53, 119–20
and shift to I/You relationship, 111–12
to signals of knee-jerk reactions, 105–106, 108
to silence versus activity in conversations, 120
to talking-listening balance in communication, 120
techniques for, 112–21
watching versus, 78
Peace process, 58–60, 63–64, 68, 74, 93–94
Personality and physical characteristics, 41–42
Peters, Tom, 172, 191–92
Physical characteristics and personality, 41–42
Physical reactions
knee-jerk reactions and, 105
muscle tension, 105
paying attention to, 105, 164–66
pulse rate, 105
Piatigorsky, Gregor, 164
Plato, 90

Please Understand Me (Kiersey and Bates), 197
PLO, 63–64, 68, 74
Polarity Management (Johnson), 143
Politics, 70–71
Porter, Elias, 212 (ch6,n6)
Poseidon Adventure, 96
Positions versus issues, 69, 71–72
Power of Nice (Shapiro), 73
Presentations
    conversation versus, 34, 43–44
    mistakes in, 111, 114–15
Prince (Machiavelli), 70
Prison experiment, 88–89
Problem solving versus litigation, 69

Quality improvement, 47–48, 83
Qurei, Ahmed. *See* Ala, Abu

Rackham, Neil, 120, 136, 147–49
Rank and status, 87–88, 96, 201–203
Reactions. *See also* Physical reactions
    to anxiety, 97–99
    and bad timing issues, 85, 104, 188–89
    conflicts between ideas, 83–84
    and connection with others' goals, 145
    context and, 82–85
    exploration of others' reactions, 53–54, 56, 123–38
    fear response, 36–39, 43–46, 54, 84, 94–95, 125, 129, 139, 164
    and history of the idea, 83
    to ideas, 26–27, 29, 31, 45, 82–85
    knee-jerk reactions, 44–46, 51–52, 93–108
    missing others' reactions to ideas, 22–23
    negative emotional reactions and resistance, 33–34, 36–39, 43–46
    paying attention to, 52–53, 119–20
    principles of engagement for building favorable reactions, 49–57

resilience versus burnout, 84–85, 189
Reciprocity, 98, 128
Ka ional therapy, 136–38
Relationship-based exchanges, 175, 176
Relationships. *See also* Communication; Engagement principles
    beliefs and, 90–91, 92, 173–75
    benefits of building lasting relationships, 188
    and change generally, 13–15
    clear intention and, 49–50, 56
    cultural differences in, 175
    distrust within, 33–34, 39–46, 85–91, 100–101, 103
    environment and, 88–90
    erosion in, 118
    excitement and, 176–77
    family relationships, 195–206
    fear response and, 37–39, 43–46, 54, 125, 129, 139
    forgiveness and, 41, 108, 181, 183–85
    frozen state, 99
    group representation and lack of trust, 41–42, 86, 190
    history together and lack of trust, 40–41, 86
    I/It relationship, 64, 65–69, 70, 108, 174, 196–204
    I/You relationship, 64–65, 67–78, 102, 106–107, 108, 111–12, 131–32, 174, 176, 188
    I/you relationship, 97–98, 102
    i/YOU relationship, 98, 102
    i/you relationship, 98–99, 102
    importance of work relationships, 169
    intention and focus on, 74
    and leaning in and leaning away movements, 113–15, 119
    missed signals and, 109–10
    parent-child relationship, 132, 134, 164, 171, 177–78, 195, 196–204
    rank and status, 87–88, 96, 201–203

relationship-based exchanges, 175, 176
repairing damaged relationships generally, 188
repairing Level 3 mistrust, 177–78, 181–82
self-assessment on, 110, 179–80
and settling for less, 192
shift from I/It to I/You relationship, 68–77, 106–107, 108, 111–12
struggle of, 170–75
taking responsibility in, 181
techniques for building stronger relationships, 172
and transaction-based exchanges, 170–71, 173, 175–76
trust and, 29–31, 45
Relaxation, 104, 155–58
Relaxation Response (Benson), 155–56
Relaxed concentration, 118–19, 154
Reno, Janet, 54
Representation of groups, 41–42, 86, 190
Republic (Plato), 90
Reputation, loss of, 96
Resilience, 84–85, 211 (ch5,n6)
Resistance. *See also* Engagement principles
    avoidance of, 169–85
    and burnout versus resilience, 84–85, 189
    causes of, 14, 33–34, 46
    conversation versus presentation in dealing with, 34, 43–44
    dealing with Level 2 and Level 3 resistance, 43–46
    lack of trust and, 33–34, 39–46
    and lack of understanding, 33–36, 45, 46
    levels of, 33–46, 82–91
    negative emotional reactions and, 33–34, 36–39, 43–46
    positive aspects of, 170
    to quality improvement, 47–48

questions on, 46
  recognition of levels of, 42
Rhino Foods, 142–43
Ripken, Cal, Jr., 73
Rogers, Carl, 110–11
Ruffalo, Mark, 163

Sabotage, 118
Safety issues, 98–99, 125, 131–32
Sales, 81–82, 85, 120, 136,
  147–49, 164, 171
Savir, Uri, 63–64, 68, 74
School system, 24–25, 26, 31
Schopenhauer, Arthur, 57
Sereny, Gitta, 117
Shapiro, Ron, 73
Simon, Neil, 117
Social Animal (Aronson), 80–81
South Africa, 79–80, 181
Spector, Phil, 120
Speer, Albert, 117
SPIN Selling (Rackham), 147
Sports, 52, 67
Stanford prison experiment,
  88–89
Stanislavski, Konstantin, 73
Star Trek, 91
Status and rank, 87–88, 96,
  201–203
Stay versus leave decision,
  189–92
Stevenson, Adlai, 139
Stranger in a Strange Land
  (Heinlein), 132
Summerall, Pat, 52
Sun Tzu, 70
Sweeney, John, 178

T'ai Chi, 157
Taking breaks, 106–107, 166–67
Taking responsibility, 181
Teenagers, 132, 134, 197–98
Telemarketing, 49–52
Television, 107, 121, 126, 195
Tennis, 118–19, 154
Theater improvisation work, 75,
  77, 88, 115–16. *See also*
  Actors
Threats, 97, 191
Timing issues, 85, 104, 188–89

TM (transcendental
  meditation), 155
Toscanini, Arturo, 164
Transaction-based exchanges,
  170–71, 173, 175–76
Transcendental meditation
  (TM), 155
Trust
  beliefs and relationships,
    90–91, 92
  and connection with others'
    goals, 145
  context and, 85–91
  cultural background and lack
    of, 42
  environment and relation-
    ships, 88–90
  and exploring differences, 133
  and finding common con-
    cerns, 178
  forgiveness and, 181, 183–85
  group representation and lack
    of, 41–42, 86, 190
  history together and lack of,
    40–41, 86
  and I/You relationship, 177, 182
  ideas and, 29–31, 45
  information access and,
    181–82
  keeping commitments and,
    178, 181
  knee-jerk reactions and dis-
    trust, 100–101, 103
  lack of, and resistance, 33–34,
    39–46
  listening and, 182
  making the first move for
    repairing mistrust,
    177–78
  and peace process in Northern
    Ireland, 60
  principles of engagement for
    building, 49–57
  and relative rank and status,
    87–88
  repairing relationships of mis-
    trust, 177–78, 181–82
  taking responsibility and, 181
  value differences and lack of,
    42–43

Unburdened Heart (Nelson),
  183–85
Understanding
  agreement versus, 26
  and connection with others'
    goals, 145
  and exploring differences,
    127–30, 133
  of ideas, 25–26, 31, 45
  lack of, and resistance, 33–36,
    45, 46
  principles of engagement for
    building favorable reac-
    tions, 49–57
  relational therapy and, 137
Union and management bargaining, 71–72, 192
Ury, William, 69, 71–72

Values
  attack on, 96, 190–91
  differences in, and lack of
    trust, 42–43
Vanderbilt University, 103
Vietnam War, 43
Vivian, C. T., 103

Waldmeir, Patti, 79
Wallace, George, 41
Wallen, Richard, 212 (ch6,n6)
Ward, Jason, 146
Waterman, Robert, 172, 192
West, Mae, 47
West Side Story, 20–21
Whistler, James McNeill, 109
Wilde, Oscar, 33
Winfrey, Oprah, 73
Winning
  small wins and longer-term
    goals, 192
  win-win, 146
  winning at all costs, 96
Wood, Robert, 96
Worst-case scenarios, 129

Yontef, Gary, 136, 169
"You Bet Your Life," 107
You Can Count on Me, 163

Zimbardo, Philip, 88–89